Delaware River

America's Historic, Scenic, and Working Waterway

by

John Bernardo

HERITAGE BOOKS
2016

HERITAGE BOOKS
AN IMPRINT OF HERITAGE BOOKS, INC.

Books, CDs, and more—Worldwide

For our listing of thousands of titles see our website
at
www.HeritageBooks.com

Published 2016 by
HERITAGE BOOKS, INC.
Publishing Division
5810 Ruatan Street
Berwyn Heights, Md. 20740

Copyright © 2016 John Bernardo

Heritage Books by the author:
Delaware River: America's Historic, Scenic, and Working Waterway
Hudson River: A Scenic and Historic Natural Treasure

All rights reserved. No part of this book may be reproduced or transmitted in any form or by any means, electronic or mechanical, including photocopying, recording or by any information storage and retrieval system without written permission from the author, except for the inclusion of brief quotations in a review.

International Standard Book Numbers
Paperbound: 978-0-7884-5712-8
Clothbound: 978-0-7884-6428-7

Table of Contents

PREFACE	5
DELAWARE RIVER	7
Upper Delaware	22
Middle Delaware	32
Lower Delaware	38
Delaware Valley, Kittatinny Mountain Region and Delaware River Highlands	48
Some Tributaries	53

CHAPTER 1   65
Wetlands, aquatic plants, fish, other wildlife, and its overall ecosystem

CHAPTER 2   87
Delaware River's pollution issues, preventive measures/solutions and flood/climate change concerns

CHAPTER 3
Crossings (Bridges) of the Delaware River   101

CHAPTER 4   111
Trails (Water and Land), greenways, parks, historic attractions and recreation on the Delaware River

CHAPTER 5   139
Some historical highlights of the Delaware River itself, its navigational system, towns, region, geology, landscape, and ecosystem

AUTHOR'S SUMMARY   157

PREFACE

Writing has been my passion since 1988 when I became a freelance journalist. So far, I have written over 600 articles. Some of these stories were published in newspapers; the rest in magazines. I addition to my articles, I am the proud, published author of four books. Of course, *Delaware River* represents my most recent, fifth published book. Before *Delaware River*, my latest book was on the Hudson River that was published in 2013.

What inspired me to write about the Delaware River was when I lived in New Jersey from 1982 to 1984. During that time, I served in the U.S. Air Force and was stationed at McGuire Air Force Base in Wrightstown, New Jersey. And since McGuire Air Force Base was relatively close to Trenton, I would travel over the Trenton Bridge and end up in Morrisville, Pennsylvania. From Morrisville, I would drive on Route 32, also known as River Road, along the Lower Delaware River. Along the way, I saw interesting, unique cliffs on my left and a shallow, rocky, river on my right as I passed Yardley, Washington Crossing and Bowman's Tower before I spent time in New Hope in Bucks County, Pennsylvania.

Then during the early 1990s, I returned to the Northeast and was trained as an Assistant Conductor with Amtrak in Washington, D.C. While in Washington, I would sometimes travel by train to Trenton, New Jersey. While in Trenton, I made my way back to Route 32 and enjoyed the scenery of both the Pennsylvania and New Jersey sides of the Delaware River. The Delaware's natural beauty, unique geology, importance as a transportation artery, scenic attractions, and epic history are five, key traits that sparked me to learn more about the river and then write about it.

The main purpose of my book is to educate readers on the Delaware River as an important natural resource, show them how it provides people with many recreational opportunities, have readers understand its critical impact on the local and national economy, and explain to those interested how the river represents a huge part of America's history.

What makes my book about the Delaware different from other books written on the subject is that *Delaware River* doesn't focus on just one aspect or characteristic of the river. My book reaches out to readers as it provides them with a general guide and/or better overall understanding of the Delaware. When people read my book they will obtain valuable information about its tributaries, region, ecosystem, pollution issues, and crossings. My work titled *Delaware River* also shows us how important the Delaware River is as a crucial, natural resource used by fish, other wildlife, and humans. Finally, my book is also a guide for residents and visitors that wish to participate in recreation and see or experience the river's greenways, trails, parks, and other attractions.

    I am dedicating *Delaware River* to nature lovers, river advocates, and history buffs. A special dedication goes out to my daughters, Michelle and Melissa Bernardo, who like myself, find the Delaware River and other rivers interesting. We appreciate and enjoy rivers, such as the Delaware River, because rivers provide habitat to a variety of life forms and benefit the quality of life for different civilizations.

DELAWARE RIVER

The Delaware River is the longest, free-flowing river in the eastern United States. For the most part, the condition of the Delaware River is a product of the cumulative flows from its numerous tributaries. Meanwhile, the Delaware's tributaries take their character from the underlying topography, geology, microclimates, and land uses of their watersheds.

All along the Delaware between Trenton, New Jersey and the Delaware Bay are different marinas and associated facilities. For instance, on the Pennsylvania side, there are remnants of the industrial age, including the old U.S. Steel Plant in Fairless Hills, as well as docks that were used to offload coal and other raw materials. Head north of Trenton and look towards the New Jersey side where you will see a lot of scenic landscape.

In addition to its picturesque terrain, the Delaware River is a diverse river, being one of nine "Great Waters" recognized by the America's Great Waters Coalition (an alliance of national, regional, state, and local organizations working to protect, preserve, and restore our country's Great Waters). In its northern, nature-oriented stretch, the river runs freely and swiftly supplying clean drinking water to millions of people (including many New York City residents) as it moves past woodlands, farmlands, and villages. In its southern portion as it moves toward Philadelphia, Pennsylvania, the Delaware becomes a mighty, industrial, commerce-bound river running parallel to some of the most densely populated urban areas in America.

Besides having two identities, this free-moving, pristine river also creates the political boundary between New York and Pennsylvania, New Jersey and Pennsylvania, and New Jersey and Delaware. In fact, these four states (Delaware, New Jersey, New York, and Pennsylvania) have argued over control of the Delaware River's resources since shortly after General George Washington crossed it in 1776.

Yet the Delaware is so much more than a historic river that Washington crossed. For generations, the Delaware River has been home to canoes and steamboats, fishermen and swimmers, and factories and shipyards. Furthermore, industry and recreation have coexisted for many decades along the Delaware's changing banks.

In fact, the most symbolic rivers in New Jersey are the Delaware and Hudson. The Delaware River structures the state's entire western border with Pennsylvania and most of its border with Delaware. The Hudson River is the natural border between northeastern New Jersey and New York.

Rivers have a splendor that is all their own, especially rivers like the Delaware. It's not majestic like the Hudson, but it is modest, surging above the tops of hidden boulders, rolling into a churning wake or silently moving with a silvery shine over a bed of pebbles.

Yet by far the most scenic portions of the Delaware are in the Catskill Mountains between New York and Pennsylvania (known as the Upper Delaware) and the region between New Jersey and Pennsylvania, which form the Delaware Water Gap National Recreation Area (Central Delaware Region).

The Delaware River corridor also offers scenic autumn foliage, dramatic natural ice sculptures in the winter, and the natural migration of birds in the spring. The scenery of the historic riverside mills and towns compliments spectacular views of the river and canals. Both New Jersey and Pennsylvania have designated the routes that flank the Delaware as scenic byways.

Scenery of the Delaware River is what attracted some famous artists to the region. One artist that comes to mind is Frank Schoonover. Some of his paintings included the Delaware River Region's industrial landscape in the 1900s and the pristine vistas of the Delaware River in the 1930s. Schoonover's sketches of boys working in coalmines and girls laboring in textile mills, and his oil paintings of panoramic river settings in the Pocono Mountains in Pennsylvania, are art that portrays issues of human rights and environmentalism.

Schoonover grew up in the town of Bushkill, near the Delaware River in Pike County, Pennsylvania where his drawings of streams, rivers and bridges matured into imitations of illustrations made by Howard Pyle who became America's foremost illustrator at the end of the 19th century. In 1914, Schoonover purchased his own art studio in Bushkill and eventually he made well over 200 paintings of the Delaware River.

Digressing to the river's history, Dutch explorers named the Delaware the South River to distinguish it from the North River, an estuary of the Hudson River. Known to many as a

"Servant of many masters," the Delaware's uses consist of industrial plants, shipping, recreation, and drinking water.

For a river that isn't very wide, the Delaware transports a powerful lot of water. In fact, its 13,000 square mile watershed includes 216 tributaries. The river's tributaries begin in the Pocono Mountains in Pennsylvania and Catskill Mountains in New York. The Catskill Watersheds provide a prime source of high quality water and New York City obtains more than half of its water supply (even though the headwaters of the Delaware do not naturally flow to New York City) from the Upper Delaware River Basin.

Although the Delaware River Watershed drains only about 4 percent of the continental United States, the watershed and its 216 tributaries provide 700 million gallons of drinking water daily for over 17 million people in portions of New York, New Jersey, Pennsylvania, and Delaware (including many urban areas such as New York City and Philadelphia).

Lying in the densely populated corridor of the northeastern U.S., the Delaware River Basin stretches approximately 330 miles from its headwaters in New York State to its confluence with the sea. Furthermore, about 90% of all water withdrawn from the Delaware Basin is diverted from surface water flows. Potable water in the basin is supplied from surface water diversions (64%) and ground water withdrawals (36%). Almost 90% of all potable supply for residential and commercial use is through public water supply systems and just 10% is from domestic (household) wells.

In addition to drinking, the Delaware is the water source for cooking, washing, industrial, watering and agricultural uses. Furthermore, the Delaware River Watershed provides a world-class trout fishery.

The Delaware originates as fresh water in the western Catskill Mountains of New York State in the East Branch and West Branch Rivers that meet close to Hancock, New York. From that point, the river moves south 280 miles to Delaware Bay on the Atlantic Ocean. The same river that flows through the gills of a rainbow trout in Hancock, past the rural town of Easton, Pennsylvania and over the short hills of Trenton, New Jersey, will later pass the refinery towns of Marcus Hook, Pa. and splash against cargo ships at the Port of Wilmington, Delaware.

A great part of the Delaware River is represented by the Delaware River Water Trail. The Water Trail encompasses about 200 miles of the whole freshwater portion of the Delaware River, from Hancock, New York down to the Trenton, New Jersey/Morrisville, Pennsylvania region. The Delaware River Water Trail consists of guided access points and day use and/or camping sites for boaters. It also provides one-stop trip planning information that considers the Delaware River as a whole system, shows boaters where and how to navigate it safely, and advises people on ways to help safeguard its resources.

And as I mentioned earlier, along the Delaware's path it forms the boundary separating Pennsylvania from New York and New Jersey and separates Delaware from New Jersey. After passing the plateau and mountains, the river winds down deep Appalachian valleys and runs around the Kittatinny range, which it crosses at the Delaware Water Gap. From the Gap (the Middle Delaware), the river flows between nearby vertical walls of limestone and rolls through a charming and tranquil country of woodland and farmland, diversified with long cliffs and plateaus, until it crosses the Appalachian plain and enters the hills again at Easton, Pennsylvania.

When its East and West Branches join, the Delaware River is 224 miles long to tidewater, followed by 96 miles of estuary. The Delaware Estuary, which is about 133 miles long, is a tidally dominated system where its tidal flow is 300 times its freshwater flow. The tide ranges in height, on average, from 4.25 feet at the confluence with the Atlantic Ocean to 8.25 feet at the head of tide in Trenton, New Jersey.

In regards to the river's salinity, salinity is a controlling factor for the estuary's ecology. The interaction of the tidal flow from the Atlantic and the freshwater flows from the primary stem Delaware River and its tributaries cause the salinity distribution in the Delaware Estuary. The biggest changes in salinity are within the transition zone between the Delaware River and the Atlantic Ocean.

As the Delaware heads downstream away from its upper portion, the river begins to slice through the Appalachian Mountains at the Delaware Water Gap (Middle Delaware) near Stroudsburg, Pennsylvania, and next the estuary becomes deeper, navigable and tidal at Morrisville, Pennsylvania and Trenton, New

Jersey. At Trenton, there is a fall of eight feet and the Port of Trenton is known as "the Falls of the Delaware," which is the highest navigable point on the Delaware River.

Underneath Trenton, the Delaware moves south between Philadelphia and New Jersey before it reaches its mouth. As the Delaware River flows past Trenton, freshwater starts to mix with saltwater from the Delaware Bay, creating the Delaware Estuary. At its mouth, it becomes a deep, sluggish inlet of the sea, with marshes along its side, widening steadily into the Delaware Bay (its estuary) to finish its 331-mile journey.

Another interesting characteristic about the Delaware River is that it huddles close together to other major rivers in the Northeast. The Delaware (New York, New Jersey, Pa. and Del.), Hudson (New York and New Jersey), Susquehanna (Pa.), and Potomac (Va., D.C. and Md.) all lie within 225 miles of each other at their mouths.

The river's total length, from the head of the longest branch to the capes (Cape May and Cape Henlopen in New Jersey), is 410 miles and over the head of the bay its length is 360 miles. The Delaware River's deepest point is at Narrowsburg, New York (Upper Delaware) where it's 113 feet deep. Historians believe that the Delaware at Narrowsburg is a "plunge pool" created from a glacial waterfall. The average freshwater discharge of the Delaware River into the lower end of the river is 11,550 cubic feet per second.

The condition of the Delaware River is a product of the cumulative flows from its many tributaries that in turn take their character from the underlying topography, geology, microclimates and land uses of their watersheds. The Delaware River's northernmost tributaries originate in the forested western slopes of the Catskill Mountains that reach elevations of up to 4,000 feet. The river later descends approximately 800 feet on its journey to the Atlantic Ocean.

The main tributaries of the Delaware are the Lehigh and Schuylkill Rivers in Pennsylvania, the Neversink and Mongaup Rivers in New York, and the Musconetcong and Maurice Rivers in New Jersey. As for the Delaware River, it has no real waterfalls along it. However, along the tributaries of the Delaware River in northeastern Pennsylvania there are many scenic waterfalls. As water drains down the Poconos and other mountains in the region on the way to the Delaware River, the water falls over many ledges, cliffs and escarpments (steep slopes or cliffs) making some tall and spectacular waterfalls for visitors and hikers to see in Pennsylvania.

Moving on to the Upper Delaware River Estuary, it is mainly made up of freshwater. Although the transition point between salt water and freshwater moves depending upon rainfall and in drought conditions, brackish water can flow upstream. The location of salt water fluctuates along the tidal Delaware River as stream flows increase or decrease in response to changes in concentrating chlorides or inflows in the river.

When crossing the Delaware, pedestrians, bicyclists, and motorists will see that the river is a main barrier to travel between New Jersey and Pennsylvania. Most of the bigger bridges are strictly tolled westbound and are owned by the Delaware River Port Authority, Delaware River and Bay Authority, Burlington Bridge Commission or the Delaware River Joint Toll Bridge Commission.

In regards to flooding, just like how other rivers in the Northeast flood, the Delaware River has flooded many times due to snow melting and/or rain run-off from severe rainstorms. One flood that stands out in particular was the June 2006 flood. During that flood, rain fell over the Delaware River Basin every day from June 23 to June 28, 2006. Total precipitation ranged from 3 to 6.5 inches across the New Jersey portion of the basin and most flooding in New Jersey occurred along the mainstream of the Delaware River. Besides New Jersey, 7 to 15 inches of rainfall were recorded in northeastern Pennsylvania. In addition, the New York section of the basin received 6 to 14 inches during the same period.

In general, flooding in the upper portion of the Delaware Basin affects mostly natural unpopulated flood plains. But flooding has recently damaged the land and homes of residents in the middle Delaware Basin.

In April 2011, the states of Delaware, New Jersey, Pennsylvania, and New York accepted a plan that will help reduce the threat of flooding along the Delaware. Regarding the plan, New York City (NYC) has agreed to change the amount of water released from its reservoir system (three reservoirs) in the Catskill Region in New York State located in the headwaters area of the

Delaware River. These three NYC reservoirs can hold over 276 billion gallons of water.

By implementing this change, New York City would provide drought relief and flood protection. Utilities that purchase water will then be able to tap into a bigger share of the Delaware River water through the Delaware and Raritan Canal. New York City will test a method to help to prevent threats of flooding down the river by maintaining reservoirs below capacity when the risk of flood downstream is greatest.

As for the Lower Delaware Basin (Philadelphia southward to the Delaware Bay), that is tidal and much wider than portions further north and therefore is not inclined to river related flooding (yet tidal surges can cause minor flooding in that region).

The Delaware River Basin Commission (DRBC) and local governments are addressing the issue of flooding along the river. The past few years have seen an increase in fatal floods and most river residents want something to be done. The DRBC is also addressing the issue of climate change and how that may cause the level of precipitation to likely continue frequent flooding in the Delaware River Valley.

Many scientists and environmentalists have concluded that the effects of climate change will impact the Delaware River Basin. Meanwhile, in addition to frequent flooding and participation, scientists and other experts claim global warming will increase temperatures in the Delaware River's estuary and valley, resulting in earlier springs and warmer winters. They also claim global warming will make the sea level rise.

A rise in sea level of just one foot would have huge impacts on flooding, coastal erosion, and saltwater intervention. Since the late 1970s, the Delaware River Basin Commission (DRBC) has analyzed the implications of recent sea level trends in its policy making. In fact, researchers predict that saltwater encroachment likely caused from sea level surge in the next century is due to the expected global warming.

In the Delaware Estuary, tidal effects extend as far upriver as Trenton, New Jersey, where the tidal range is more than two times that of the ocean boundary. Even though the net flow of the estuary tends to bring salt water toward the ocean, tidal currents carry salt water upriver, where it mixes with fresh water. The differences in the densities of salt water and fresh water also contribute to saltwater intrusion; heavy salt water on the bottom typically flows upriver when next to lighter fresh water, creating a wedge.

An increase in sea level normally results in increased salinity as long as other factors remain constant. In this situation the impact of sea level rise is like the impact of decreased flow during a drought. The former increases the saltwater force, whereas the later decreases the freshwater force. Typically, salinity levels respond to changes in tide and river flow within minutes or hours.

Data found by researchers and scientists show that in the past 18,000 years, sea level ascended three hundred feet, converting freshwater rivers into brackish estuaries. The Delaware Estuary and Chesapeake Bay are examples of such drowned river valleys. The Delaware Estuary is probably the first estuary for which the salinity effects of future sea level rise has been studied. Since the early 1930s, the salinity of the Delaware Estuary, as affected by the impacts of river diversion and flow regulation projects, has been the topic of study and litigation.

In regards to an excess amount of salt found in the Delaware River, an increase in sea level of several feet would greatly aggravate the present salinity problems in the Delaware Estuary. The upper estuary above the Schuylkill River (main tributary of the Delaware River) in Philadelphia, now a source of fresh water for both cities and industries, would become too salty for most uses, forcing a switch to alternative supplies at a huge expense. Philadelphia's water supply intake at Torresdale (a neighborhood in the far Northeast section of the city), now in the freshwater portion of the estuary, would be subject to occasional invasions of sea salts that would sometimes leave the water unacceptable for the city's many water customers. After the sea level increases, industries currently using fresh water from the upper estuary would see brackish water at their intakes during dry periods. Those industries presently using brackish water from the middle and lower sections of the estuary would have much higher salinities than those for which their systems were designed, which would damage tanks, pipes, and machinery, and boost water treatment costs. In some instances, these industries would need to permanently shift to alternative water supplies.

Furthermore, ecologists are concerned about potential impacts of increased salinities on estuarine plants and animals of the Delaware River Region. The magnitude of salinity increase found in the Delaware River Basin Commission models of postulated accelerated rises in sea level would make great changes in the ecology of the Delaware Estuary. There would be an up-estuary advance of estuarine and marine species and a retreat of freshwater species. Hence, some species currently thriving in clean waters of the lower estuary would migrate into the more polluted reaches of the upper estuary, closer to wastewater outfalls and other hazards. Today, vessels using the freshwater portions of the upper estuary would experience problems due to marine fouling organisms. The marine organisms would also infest water systems that take water from the tidal river in areas of the Delaware now free of this problem.

In addition to the environmental impact of salinities to the Delaware Estuary, higher water levels caused by an increasing sea level could drown a lot of the approximate 320 square miles of wetlands along the Delaware River. Fortunately, the wetlands that supply crucial habitats for numerous species of fish and birds are protected partially from present human interference by state and federal laws. But even though these laws are in place, ecosystems have the potential to migrate landward with an increasing sea level. This migration can remove one of nature's cleansing mechanisms in which a loss of wetlands could increase pollution loadings in the Delaware Estuary.

Digressing to climate change, the Delaware River is now warming and the consequences could affect the quality of the drinking water, fishing, and other assets this scenic river provides to millions of people. Waterways in urban areas show the highest temperature increases. Hence, researchers found that the temperature in the Delaware is experiencing the fastest rise among 20 American rivers, including the Hudson and Potomac. Warmer temperatures in the Delaware can spark the growth of invasive species such as algae. These temperatures can also affect toxicity levels, an issue in any body of water used for drinking.

Moreover, a local river agency named Partnership for the Delaware Estuary, reported in 2010 that climate change would affect the Delaware Estuary over the next few decades. The report by the Partnership for the Delaware Estuary indicated that climate change would consist of warmer temperatures and stronger storms.

The report also predicted an increase in median temperature of four to seven degrees Fahrenheit over the next ninety years. That increase in temperature would translate into a rise in sea level between 1.5 and 5 feet, which would increase the volume of salt water in the Delaware River in the next century. If no countermeasures are taken, a repeat of the 1960s' drought with a 2.4-foot rise would send the salt front upriver to river-mile 100, compared with mile 93 for the current sea level.

Meanwhile, the Partnership is now acting upon potential future climate changes and its report outlines steps to lessen the impact of climate change over the next 100 years including preserving land bordering tidal wetlands and giving wetlands an undeveloped space to move to if the sea level rises. Finally, the report advocates more preservation of forestland in northeastern Pennsylvania and southern New York as part of an effort to ensure clean drinking water into the future.

In regards to the area's environment, lifestyle, and economy, the upper and central Delaware is home to many fish, birds (resident and migratory species) and other wildlife. Digressing to the river's salinity distribution, the distribution of salinity affects the aquatic and wetland habitats that exist and the species that live in these habitats.

The Delaware River provides habitat for 15 species of waterfowl and is a vital component of the Atlantic Flyway, one of four primary waterfowl routes in North America. In addition, the estuary is home to more than 30 species of mammals and reptiles.

In fact, there are twelve species of marine mammals that are known to migrate into the Atlantic Ocean close to the Delaware Estuary Region. The most common species are the harbor porpoise, bottlenose dolphin, harbor seal, gray seal, and humpback whale. Other species sometimes seen are the harp seal, hooded seal, ringed seal, pygmy sperm whale, fin whale and northern right whale. Typically using offshore areas, the different mammals occasionally have been found in open water from the mouth of the Delaware Bay up into river channels.

The Delaware River serves as a feeding ground for marine mammals, providing an abundance of preferred fish species and crustaceans. The Delaware also provides some shelter from big predators and harsh weather conditions offshore. It also attracts a very large concentration of migrating shore birds and both the upper and middle parts of the river provide a scenic landscape where residents can enjoy a rural lifestyle.

Economically on local, national, and global levels, there are many economic benefits from the Delaware River. When you travel downstream, you will see that the Lower Delaware and its estuary host an active commercial fishery, along with the Port of Philadelphia, which is the biggest freshwater port complex in the world and a major port of entry. The Delaware River Port Complex is one of only 14 strategic ports in America transporting military equipment and supplies by vessel to support our troops overseas. Each year, the Philadelphia Port (commercial lane in Penn's Landing area is 400 feet wide) handles several thousand cargo ships from around the globe. Like the Hudson River, the Delaware is a "working" waterway or "urbanized and commercialized" river.

Moreover, along the Philadelphia waterfront are many facilities for refining sugar and petroleum, generating electricity, and producing and distributing goods. The Lower Delaware also provides jobs for many people, as more than 3,000 deep draft ships enter the estuary every year to deliver cargo. Further upstream, the Delaware still holds a deep shipping channel and it's not uncommon to see a giant freighter moving up river to unload its cargo at a port in southern Bucks County, Pennsylvania.

The Delaware River Area represents the fourth-busiest port for water traffic in the United States and the Delaware River ranks second only to the Mississippi River among American rivers in the amount of commerce it transports each year. In its 60-mile industrialized stretch from Trenton, New Jersey through Philadelphia, Pa. to Wilmington, Del., the Lower Delaware River hauls over 75% as much tonnage as the Mississippi (not including its tributaries) carries in over 2,000 miles from Minneapolis, Minnesota to the Gulf of Mexico.

Ranked number one among U.S. rivers for its import tonnage, the Delaware brings giant tankers from the Middle East to oil refineries around Philadelphia and gives large freighters access to the chemical work facilities at Wilmington, Del. Almost 42 million gallons of crude oil are moved on the Delaware River on a daily basis. It is also the biggest receiving port in the U.S. for very large Crude Carriers (tank ships weighing more than 125,000 tons). Furthermore, about 70% of the oil that arrives on the Atlantic coast was already transported through the Delaware Estuary. However, these statistics also indicate there is a high risk for oil spills in this region.

Furthermore, the Delaware River Port Complex is home to the hugest North American Port for steel, meat, and paper imports as well as the largest importer of fruit and cocoa beans on the East Coast. Over 65% of South American fruits imported into the United States arrive in terminal facilities in the tri-state (Pennsylvania, New Jersey, and Delaware) port complex. And Wilmington, Delaware is home to the biggest U.S. banana importing port, handling over 1 million tons of this cargo annually from Central America.

Indeed, the Delaware River has a huge economic impact in New Jersey, Pennsylvania and Delaware. Meanwhile in June 2011, researchers from the University of Delaware's Water Resources Agency (WRA) measured the value of the tidal Delaware River and tributaries in three ways.

First of all, researchers found the tidal Delaware and its tributaries had an economic impact of $10 billion through economic activity from water quality, water supply, recreation, fishing, hunting, agriculture, forests and parks. Second, they discovered the Delaware helped generate $12 billion through the value of services and goods provided by the estuary's ecosystems (such as flood reduction and water filtration). Finally, researchers measured the economic value of the river in a third way when they found the Delaware River pumped $10 billion into the region's economy through employment. This employment included over 500,000 direct and indirect jobs with annual wages in the farm, coastal, water/wastewater, ecotourism, recreation and port industries.

As for river recreation, some activities people engage in, on, and/or near the river include hiking, biking, boating, fishing, swimming, and bird watching. Besides recreation, the Delaware is rich in history. From its headwaters to its mouth, the estuary is full of cultural, natural, and archeological treasures. Some of these treasures consist of historic canals, Native American and colonial sites, towns comprised of antique architecture, revolutionary era buildings, and 19th century mills.

Looking back to its early stages of development, the Delaware Estuary was originally created after flooding of the coastal plain by the Delaware River after the last ice age. The estuary is a "drowned" river valley, or a valley previously at sea level that has become submerged.

Besides its history, the Delaware Estuary's wetlands are vitally significant to the long-term health of an array of life forms. The Delaware River Estuary is lined with critical wetlands that filter sediments and pollutants from the land and act as buffers that protect the waterway from erosion and flooding.

The estuary has 405,000 acres of habitat that includes over 126,000 acres, which are recognized as globally significant. It's also home to the biggest population of horseshoe crabs in the world plus it provides habitat to over 130 species of fish as well as oysters, clams, other crabs, diamondback terrapins, and duck.

Regarding its physical characteristics, the 133-mile-long Delaware Estuary is a tidally dominated system, where the tidal flow is 300 times the freshwater flow. Its tide ranges in height, on average, from 4.25 feet at the confluence with the Atlantic Ocean to 8.25 feet at the head of tide in Trenton, New Jersey.

In addition to the Delaware River's physical characteristics, beauty, economic value, ecological importance, and other important traits it possesses in the region, its geology, geologic history, and sedimentation are all environmentally and naturally significant, have truly unique characteristics and beautify the area. Furthermore, the geologic history of the Delaware River is rich and interesting to many people that include sightseers, hikers, boaters, anglers, historians, geologists, wildlife officials, and scientists.

In regards to geology, drive north along Route 29 to Stockton, New Jersey and you will see an exposure of the fanglomerate of the Stockton Formation, which consists of coarse red sandstone and a sandy shale that occur in weathered road cuts and throughout active and abandoned quarries in the Stockton Region. The sandstone exposed here is called arkose that is made of coarse-sand to gravel-sized grains, has a red or pink iron-rich matrix, is rich in feldspar grains, and is derived from the fast disintegration of granite rocks.

North of Stockton, the quality of the sedimentary rock changes to a dark gray color, alternating between fine-grained sandstone and shale. These rocks occur in cliffy roadside exposures near Byram, New Jersey, which is north of Stockton. These stones represent part of the Late Triassic Lockatong Formation and are sediments deposited in a great lake, which flooded the mid-section of the Newark Basin during the Late Triassic period. The alternation between sandstone and shale units indicates that the water depth of this lake fluctuated up and down cyclically.

A few miles north of Byram, New Jersey, the sediment character along the Delaware River starts to gradually change. Thin units of red sandstone start to appear between layers of darker, brownish gray sandstone and shale. As you drive northward, these red units dominate the section. The change from dark gray to red suggests the transition from lake deposits to coastline mud flats and stream deposits. These deposits are composed of sedimentary structure, which includes mud cracks and beds consisting of mud chips that were reworked into stream channel lag deposits. These red beds overtake the stratigraphic section of rock that is appropriated to the Passaic Formation and this pair of formations is shifting from one to the other. The Lockatong (gray) and Passaic (red) are sedimentary compositions that interact with each other. This alternation of sedimentary facies developed as the shoreline of the ancient lake progressed during wet times and withdrew during dry periods.

The Delaware Water Gap (Delaware River on the New Jersey/Pennsylvania border) was a critical route for early settlers that were headed west. Over geologic time the Delaware River had eroded a way through upturned layers of hard rock, and it was much easier to construct a road close to the river instead of climbing over 1,000 feet to go over the mountain.

In Philadelphia, gravel, clay, and cobblestone are still scattered throughout the city, which showcase the area's long geological history. Geologists also state that thousands of years ago, the Philadelphia "brick clay," which are pebbles and boulders of different sizes, were transported through water (probably coming from the Delaware River). The gravel underlying the brick or boulder clays is of two types, red and yellow gravel. The material in both the red and yellow gravel is about the same white quartz or quartzite. You can obviously distinguish the gravel by their color differences. Yet another way to tell the difference from each is that the red gravel contains pebbles of red shale whereas the yellow gravel is more fossiliferous, coral and shell pebbles, indicative of the waste left from some Silurian coastline.

The geologic history of the Delaware River Region is similar to that of the Hudson River's geologic past. Here is where surface layers of stone were folded into long ridges as opposed to the cracked sections of the Taconic Mountains, which represent the range of the Appalachian Mountains along New York's eastern border. A long period of erosion followed the original mountain building, which resulted in a nearly flat surface. The Delaware River matured southeastward across this flat surface.

In recent times, mild regional uplift has allowed erosion to take place again. The upturned edges of the harder rock layers in the old folds have resisted erosion and now create long ridges. Like the Delaware and Hudson rivers, there are numerous rivers and streams that developed across the old, flat surface. As erosion set in again, and if they had enough erosion power, they were able to sustain their passageways by cutting down into the firmer ridges. Thus, mountain gaps are commonplace in this region of the Appalachians.

In addition to geology, the sedimentation (mud, sand, gravel, etc.) found on the bottom of the Delaware River Estuary plays a critical role in maintaining the balance of its ecosystem.

Most of the Delaware River Estuary is erosional, containing physical mixing and remixing sediment with specific areas of deposition and non-deposition. In the upper estuary at Philadelphia and northward, the dominant substrate is gravel and sand. Then as you move down the river, the bottom type changes from coarser to finer substrates, becoming clayey silt to silt-like clay at the Delaware/Pennsylvania border.

Moreover, there has been overbank sedimentation in the Delaware River Valley during the past 6,000 years. A very thick sequence of floodplain sediments has accumulated in the Delaware River Valley by the process of overbank deposition. Textures in the sediments show that the sequence contains no point-bar deposits and is unbroken by periods of erosion. Fourteen radiocarbon dates indicate that deposition started at least 6,000 years ago and has continued to today. And since the Delaware River shifts its position laterally at a slow rate, overbank deposition becomes dominant in the construction of its floodplain.

Upper Delaware
(Includes information on Upper Delaware River Sub-basin)

The Upper Delaware River runs 73.4 miles along the New York/Pennsylvania border. The longest, free-flowing rivers in the eastern United States, the Upper Delaware features riffles (ripples in a stream), Class I (fast-moving water with riffles, small waves and few obstructions) and Class II (faster currents, straight forward rapids of moderate difficulty with passages clear) rapids interspersed with pools and eddies (little whirlpools or whirlwinds).

Unlike other major rivers on the Eastern Seaboard, man-made dams do not shackle the Upper Delaware. Moreover, there are few power plants and large factories in the upper reaches. Both facts that I mentioned above explain why the water is unusually clean and clear.

The Upper Delaware Estuary Region stretches southwestward from Trenton, New Jersey to the Pennsylvania/Delaware border, and consists of 1,743 square miles of small sub-watersheds in Pennsylvania and New Jersey. A gently sloping topography, the primary stem of the Delaware River and a diverse landscape of fields characterize the region and forests that are commonly punctuated by development, including the cities of Philadelphia, Camden, and Trenton, define this area. Riverfront industry and development, as well as many major ports, make this area a critical economic resource to Pennsylvania and New Jersey.

The Upper Delaware River Estuary is the tidally influenced area of mainly freshwater in the Delaware River. However, the salt line, or the transition point between salt water and freshwater, moves depending on precipitation and in drought conditions, brackish (part salt water, part freshwater) can flow upstream. The Delaware River's upper stretch is special in that it is the only major river in the northeastern United States that still has no dams along its main stem.

Another important aspect of the Upper Delaware River is that, for decades, it has elevated a healthy recreational economy and is known as the best freshwater fishery east of the Mississippi River. Its average depth is four to five feet, but 12 to 18-foot holes are common, and many are deeper, to 113 feet at Big Eddy at

Narrowsburg, New York. The Upper Delaware has a total elevation differential of 460 feet, more than six feet per mile, even though it is much higher in some stretches.

As for the Upper Delaware River System, it consists of the West Branch, East Branch, and one of the river's chief tributaries, the Neversink River.

The West Branch is about 90 miles long and starts at the foundation of Cannonsville Reservoir in Delaware County, New York. Along most of its journey, it slices through a mountainous area of New York in the northern Catskill Mountains. The West Branch rises in Schoharie County, New York and generally runs southwest, entering Delaware County and flowing past the New York State communities of Stamford and Delhi. In southwestern Delaware County it moves in an increasingly winding course through the mountains, generally southwest. At Stilesville, New York, the West Branch is impounded to create the Cannonsville Reservoir. At Deposit, on the border between Broome and Delaware Counties in New York State, it makes a sharp turn to the southeast and is paralleled by New York State Route 17. The West Branch joins the East Branch at Hancock, New York to form the Delaware River. For the lower six miles, it creates part of the boundary between New York and Pennsylvania.

The West Branch is a tail water fishery with cold water almost always discovered in its upper reaches, often extending the entire length of the river into the main Delaware. It has many insect hatches and the vast array of aquatic insects and tranquil flow of the river make the West Branch ideal for dry fly anglers. In addition, high water flows and an early season make for great streamer fishing.

The West Branch is also one of the best fly fishing trout streams in America, based on its deep pools and cold water springs. The trout population in this river is reproducing naturally, but during the warm months, stocked trout from warmer and smaller tributaries will look for sanctuary in its cool water.

The East Branch Delaware River is about 75 miles long in the state of New York. The East Branch is made up of two parts, the upper and lower. The upper is that part which is upriver of its junction with the Beaverkill River in the South Central part of New York State.

The Beaver Kill, which is a famous river in the Northeast, rises in western Ulster County, New York and runs almost 44 miles through the Catskill Mountains in New York until it meets the East Branch of the Delaware River. Moreover, the East Branch River is mainly a well-known destination for fly-fishing for brown trout and its upper portion normally remains cool all season. Originating at Pepacton Reservoir, another reservoir in Delaware County, New York, it is spring creek like and more overgrown than the lower portion. The East Branch rises in eastern Delaware County, New York and flows initially south and southwest, through the town of Roxbury, New York. Eventually at the town of Hancock, New York, the East Brach River flows out of Catskill Park. A few miles beneath the town of Hancock, the river turns south and meets the West Branch to create the main stem of the Delaware River.

As for the lower section of the East Branch, it is a wider and more open waterway. Fishermen can catch a variety of brown and rainbow trout here. This part of the Delaware is an early season fishery as the river water warms during the summer and sends the trout migrating to cooler water.

Another important part of the Upper Delaware River System lies in the Neversink River in New York State. The Neversink has been classified into two parts: "above the reservoir" and "below the reservoir."

The portion above the reservoir is a smaller river made up of two branches and it flows along mostly private property. The lower section, below the reservoir is a spectacular tail water fishery that consists of stocked and wild trout (rainbows and brook). The average length of the trout falls between 12 and 13 inches. The Gorge Region, also known as the Neversink River Unique Area, is highly secluded and picturesque, located near 5,000 acres of pristine woodlands.

The Catskill Mountain Area of the Upper Delaware River Basin is about a hundred miles from New York City. The Catskill Watersheds provide a superior source of quality water, and New York City gets more than half of its water supply from three main reservoirs established in tributaries of the Upper Delaware River Basin. Yet unlike the Hudson River, the Delaware River's headwaters do not naturally flow to New York City. They drain to the state of New York, Pennsylvania, New Jersey, and Delaware.

In addition, the headwaters provide a lot of water to Philadelphia and parts of New Jersey.

Besides being a vital water supply source, the Upper Delaware River flows along the Pennsylvania and New York border for 73 miles where it can be utilized by people as a tranquil float or an exciting rapids ride. Mild whitewater rapids can be found on the upper portions of the Delaware, offering novice riders an opportunity to hone upper-body maneuvers behind the oars. Along much of the Delaware River, powerful currents muscle through wide banks, making the appearance of serenity. However, rafters, kayakers and boaters in general need to be vigilant for hazards like log jams and eel weirs that can appear just under the river's smooth surface.

In addition to people riding its rapids, the Upper Delaware was appropriated as part of the National Wild and Scenic Recreational River System in 1978 because it's a beautiful natural, recreational, and historical resource that turns through uplands scenery from Hancock, New York to just south of Matamoras, Pennsylvania. Hence, it's one of only four river sections in the Northeast that was designated as part of that honorable national river system.

When boaters float upstream from the junction of the West and East Branches in the New York Appalachian Plateau, twenty-one miles south, the river flats host a wide abundance of wildlife. Further south, the branches join in Hancock, New York, to form one of the only undammed main rivers remaining in eastern America. From that point, the Delaware starts to fall quickly through riffles and rapids separated by abrupt pools.

Beneath the confluence of the east and west forks of the Delaware River, mild rapids intersperse with long stretches of smooth water. A popular day trip runs between Pond Eddy and Port Jervis in New York, where ten miles of playful rapids alternate with smooth waters suitable for fitness rowing.

At the town of Narrowsburg, New York, the Delaware River rolls in an area between the Catskill Mountains in New York and Pocono Mountains in Pa. Narrowsburg, which is located in the middle of the Upper Delaware River corridor, is surrounded by mountains, lakes, and forests. The town oversees the Big Eddy, a popular fishing spot and the deepest point (113 feet) in the Delaware River. In addition, Narrowsburg overlooks Narrowsburg

Bridge that crosses the river at its narrowest point (hence the name Narrowsburg).

Moreover, as Narrowsburg reaches its deepest point, it's bordered with high cliffs and begins its most extreme remote segment to Barryville, New York. The next seventeen miles to Matamoros are a roller coaster of rapids that in the spring can take under 5 hours for someone to swivel in a raft. A tiny bit past midway on this stretch, the Mongaup River enters the Delaware River, making huge, high standing waves prior to reaching the sensational gorge called Hawks Nest, which is 5 miles north of Port Jervis. River riders normally can enjoy this high, rushing water in the Upper Delaware from the spring until early summer.

And for three seasons out of the year, the Delaware River serves as an exciting place for kayakers to enjoy the outdoors. Winding its path from the Pocono Mountains of Pennsylvania to northern Delaware, the river's serene waters mixed with Class III rapids provide an exciting trip for experienced kayakers. On a historical note, it is interesting to know that very little has changed along the Delaware in the hundreds of years since the Indians used to float down the river, and arrowheads can still be found along the shore.

In addition to boating and other water activities, the Upper Delaware offers visitors bird watching, hiking, fishing, and hunting. Regarding our feathered friends, the Upper Delaware contains a significant segment of the Atlantic flyway. Each year, over 200 species of birds spend part of their lives in this portion of the river. Many rare bird species such as the osprey, wild turkey, merganser, bluebird, woodpecker, ruffed geese, and pheasant are located within the Upper Delaware.

During the winter, people can engage in winter sports in the Upper Delaware Area. For instance, at the Pocono Mountains in Pennsylvania, visitors and residents can enjoy nature trails on the Poconos where they can watch bald eagles and go snowmobiling. Other winter recreational activities that the Poconos and communities in New York State offer consist of skiing, snowboarding, and ice fishing.

Furthermore, many people watch birds like the blue heron and other wildlife such as a fawn by the upper part of the Delaware. In fact, the bald eagle has recently returned to this region in huge numbers. Today, eagles nest in the Upper Delaware and during the winter, these birds are frequently seen hunting close to areas of open water in the mostly frozen Delaware in New York and Pennsylvania.

The eagles enjoy migrating to the Upper Delaware River Region because it's heavily wooded and provides for ample nesting areas. Each winter, bald eagles also migrate in the region due to the three rivers that flow through the area: the Delaware, Neversink (tributary of the Delaware) and Hudson. Also each year during the months of January and February, eagle watchers can attend eagle watch weekend events that occur in this region.

Besides birds, about 45 species of fish inhabit the Upper Delaware River. Some of these fish consist of American shad, chain pickerel, large-mouth bass, and brown, rainbow, and brook trout. Since the Upper Delaware is free flowing, shads can reach their spawning grounds upriver. From West Virginia to Maine, the Delaware River is one of only two natural shad rivers.

During the spring and summer, hikers can enjoy the Tusten Mountain Trail that overlooks the Delaware River and anglers can ply the waters for trout, shad, small mouth bass and walleyed pike. In fact, the Upper Delaware River was recently ranked number 9 out of the top ten fly fishing spots in the U.S. for trout (brookies and rainbows).

Also in the spring and summer, people can swim in the Upper Delaware but they must adhere to river safety. Although the Upper Delaware River looks calm in some areas, swimmers must respect moving water. Furthermore, swimmers need to wear their life jackets while in the Delaware and must not swim alone. People also must not swim or walk across the river. The Upper Delaware River has sharp drop-offs and strong currents that make swimming more difficult with increased current and water depth.

Besides hiking, fishing, and swimming, the Upper Delaware offers people recreational opportunities for hunting (during the season) where hunters can target black bear, white tail deer, turkey, and other game.

The Upper Delaware Watershed is also home to 50 different species of mammals including bobcat, deer, muskrat, woodchuck, rabbit, opossum, bear, fox, raccoon, and beaver. Moreover, snakes (mostly nonpoisonous ones except for rattlesnakes and copperheads) live in the region. A scenic highway also follows the Delaware River along its entire Upper Section.

In addition to the river's fish, birds, and other wildlife, the vegetation within and supporting the Upper Delaware is diverse. About 1,100 plant species can be found in the Upper Delaware Region. Some of the plants include large-toothed aspen, hemlock, oak, maple, walnut, beech, pine, ash, pine, dogwood, birch, mountain laurel, wild flowers, mosses, and ferns. Trees found throughout most of the upper river corridor region consist of red oak, red maple, black cherry, walnut, sycamore and hemlock. Old and new pastures, orchards and farms are also in the area.

Besides recreational activities, diverse wildlife, and the river's unique plant species, the geology of the Upper Delaware is unique, interesting, and scenic. The Upper Delaware also has a rich geologic history. The Upper Delaware River stretches between the Catskill Mountain physiographic section and the Appalachian Plateau physiographic province. The region's rolling hills differ in elevation from 800 to 2,000 feet and are distinguished as a series of irregular and indistinct steep slopes. Relief is typically between 300 and 500 feet, although it ranges to 700 feet in a few locations.

The Delaware River's Uplands extend from the Catskill and Pocono Mountains where the river bubbles forth as cool mountain springs and trickling streams, to Hancock, New York where its East and West Branches join to create the main stem. Although the main stem of the Delaware River remains without dams, the river still has drinking water diversions. In fact, New York City has built three reservoirs in the Uplands along the East and West Branches, diverting as much water as the city legally can. New York City releases water from the reservoirs for the City of Philadelphia and other down river users. Philadelphia, along with many other river towns, draws part of its drinking water supply directly from the Delaware.

The primary stem of the Delaware River flows down to the Delaware Water Gap where it enters the Piedmont (foothills) section of the watershed. Throughout this section of river you can see many historical sites and a scenic vegetated riparian bank. The Delaware Uplands landscape shows you a contrast of farmland and villages on the valley floor with forested hills surrounding.

In addition, the Delaware River's Uplands Region is well known for the many different species of mammals and birds it supports. The Delaware River Uplands are home to 50 different species of mammals including woodchuck, opossum, raccoon, beaver, bear, deer, fox, rabbit, muskrat, and many others. The Uplands also has rare species of birds that inhabit the area. These birds include bald eagle, osprey, wild turkey, merganser, bluebird, woodpecker, pheasant and ruffed geese.

Moreover, a marked variety of unique land shapes exist throughout the river corridor. The Delaware River Gorge, located within the Uplands Region, extends from Matamoras, Pa. and continues for much of the corridor's length. The Pennsylvania Bureau of Topographic and Geologic Survey has identified the Delaware River Gorge as one of the outstanding scenic geologic features in the state. The gorge originates above Matamoras, which lies in the easternmost part of Pennsylvania, and runs north throughout most of the river segments, ranging between two and three thousand feet in width.

Geologic processes from the Delaware River Gorge left numerous economically valuable deposits, including shale, peat, sand and gravel, and bluestone. The ancient and original materials of the majority of the soils within the river corridor have been accumulated mainly through glacial action and deposited as till or outwash from receding glaciers. Gray and red sandstone, shale, and siltstone are major contributors to the soils.

In addition to its geologic history and during the 19th century, Sullivan County, New York, part of the Upper Delaware River Area, had four important industries comprised of bluestone (discovered around 1830), timber rafting, tanning and tourism.

The Upper Delaware River Region is also part of the anthracite coal region and was strategic for hauling coal from the region by rail and canal to southern states. Indeed, the Upper Delaware River Area is a blend of nature, industry, culture, and history that many people long to explore.

The Upper Delaware River Region also includes the Upper Delaware River Sub-basin. The sub-basin comprises all of Pike and parts of Lackawanna, Monroe, Northampton, and Wayne Counties in Pennsylvania. The area is mountainous with many small streams flowing east and southeast into the Delaware River. The biggest of these streams is the Lackawaxen River.

As for its recent history, the main archeological investigations in the basin happened during the 1960s and 1970s in preparation for the Tocks Island Reservoir. Many stratified prehistoric sites were excavated during this project. Thus these sites increased the knowledge of scientists and the general public regarding the Paleo-Indian, Late Archaic, Transitional, and Late Woodland Periods. About 637 archaeological sites are recorded in the Upper Delaware River Sub-basin. However, only 237 can be assigned to a specific time period.

The Paleo-Indian Period (when hunters entered North America about 17,000 years ago) represents the earliest occupation of the region, during which the Upper Delaware River Sub-basin was sparsely occupied by small groups of foragers. The climate was evolving from Ice Age conditions where plants and animals were much different in the Upper Delaware than they are today.

Only five Paleo-Indian sites have been recorded in the sub-basin. One of these is the Shawnee-Minisink Site, one of only three Paleo-Indian sites in the Commonwealth that is in a layered context. It was found about ten feet below the surface, buried by three feet of flood-deposited sand. Radiocarbon dates place the occupation at about 10,900 years ago. Tools included over 100 end scrapers and a mix of side scrapers, knives and other tools. Many of these were used to scrape wood and bone to make handles for stone tools. Some of these scrapers were also used to clean hides for clothing and shelters. Carbonized plum, grape and hackberry seeds, as well as fish bones, represent an example of a Paleo-Indian meal.

During the Early Archaic (9,000 to 8,000 BC) and Middle Archaic (8,000 to 4,500 BC) Periods, people lived in small groups, often moving their base camps to fish, hunt and gather wild plant foods. The vegetation and climate eventually took on its modern characteristics by Middle Archaic times.

Twenty-seven Early and Middle Archaic sites are recorded in the Upper Delaware River Sub-basin. The cold climate of the glacial period continued to warm, and oak, which supplied food for both humans and the deer they hunted, was a significant part of the forest. Two Early Archaic occupation zones were discovered at Shawnee-Minisink at northeastern Pennsylvania, between two and four feet beneath the surface.

The occupants utilized a larger variety of tools than during the Paleo-Indian Period, including drills, scrapers, gravers, knives, and axes. According to historians, during the Early Archaic Period, Shawnee-Minisink probably served as a base camp for extended families in the Upper Delaware Valley.

Another deeply stratified site in the Upper Delaware Area is the Sandts Eddy site (located just north of Easton, Pennsylvania) where the earliest occupation dated approximately between 9,300 and 9,420 years ago. This occupation zone produced only a handful of artifacts and was similar to the Middle Archaic occupation at Shawnee-Minisink.

Most artifacts were related to stone tool manufacturing, but one point had evidence of use both as a spear and as a knife for butchering meat. A Middle Archaic Component dating between 7,080 and 8,450 years ago contained tools used for carving antler or bone, plant food processing, and fresh hide scraping.

Population density increased during the Late Archaic Period (3,700 to 5,000 years ago). Groups of related families established base camps, which they moved less often than in earlier periods. Seed grinding tools and fishing equipment became more common and the flora, fauna, and climate were similar to the present.

About 100 Late Archaic sites are recorded in the sub-basin that represents a big increase over Early and Middle Archaic Times. Evidence of Late Archaic occupations were found buried on floodplains at the Shawnee-Minisink site and the Egypt Mills site, both are situated along the Delaware River. Yet just a few fire pits and a small number of tools have been found at these sites. In other river valleys of Pennsylvania, larger Late Archaic base camps were discovered but so far they do not seem to exist in the Upper Delaware River Valley.

Upper Delaware River where the river narrows and flows in between New York State and Pennsylvania.

Taken from the air, shooting down on the Delaware River by Randy Palmer, pilot and photographer.

Upper Delaware River where the river narrows and flows in between New York State and Pennsylvania.

Taken from the air, shooting down on the Delaware River by Randy Palmer, pilot and photographer.

Upper Delaware River. The Mid-Delaware Bridge, also known as the Port Jervis-Matamoras Bridge, crosses over the river between Port Jervis, New York and Matamoras, Pennsylvania. The bridge is the only four-lane bridge on the upper main stem of the Delaware.

Taken from the air, shooting down on the Delaware River by Randy Palmer, pilot and photographer.

Upper Delaware River. The Mid-Delaware Bridge, also known as the Port Jervis-Matamoras Bridge, crosses over the river between Port Jervis, New York and Matamoras, Pennsylvania. The bridge is the only four-lane bridge on the upper main stem of the Delaware.

Taken from the air, shooting down on the Delaware River by Randy Palmer, pilot and photographer.

Upper Delaware River where the river narrows and flows in between New York State and Pennsylvania. The bridge in the background spans over the Delaware and connects New York State with Pennsylvania.

Taken from the air, shooting down on the Delaware River by Randy Palmer, pilot and photographer.

Middle Delaware (includes Delaware Water Gap)

The Middle Delaware River is more of a solitary river experience in a natural setting. It stands apart from the Upper and Lower Delaware River portions because it is managed by the National Park Service and is mainly part of the Delaware Water Gap National Recreation Area. The definition and scenery of the river changes as it winds its way through Matamoras, Pennsylvania and Port Jervis, New York. It is here where we leave the whitewater of the upper section for a slower and wider scenic river. This scenic section of the Delaware River is an ideal area for groups of canoe campers and autumn foliage paddling trips.

For forty miles the Middle Delaware River traverses between low-forested mountains with hardly a house in sight. Then the river slashes through the mountain ridge to create the "Delaware Water Gap."

The Delaware Water Gap is a deep, narrow gorge cut through the Kittatinny Mountains east of Stroudsburg, Pennsylvania. The Delaware Water Gap accepted its namesake from the Delaware River.

Today, the Water Gap is about three miles long and has steep walls that soar over 1,200 feet on each side. Highways follow the river's pathway through the gorge. Mount Tammany stands on the New Jersey side of the gap and Mount Minsi is on the Pennsylvania side. The gap and the area surrounding it create the Delaware Water Gap National Recreation Area.

The Water Gap offers visitors a very clean Delaware River with attractive natural beauty. But for many years, people had limited access through the gorge and good transportation was needed to attract visitors from Philadelphia and New York.

It wasn't until 1846 that a road through the Gap was improved to the point that a passenger and mail stagecoach could travel. In 1856, the Southern Division of the Delaware, Lackawanna and Western Railroad was opened and a train departing New York City could be at the Delaware Water Gap rail station within 6 hours. Today, most people can visit the Gap by car traveling on better roads. After the Civil War, the Delaware Water Gap became the second biggest inland resort town in America ranking only behind Saratoga Springs, New York. By 1900, over

500,000 people were traveling to the Gap and the Pocono, Pennsylvania Region.

The geological history of the Delaware Water Gap is also long and rich. In fact, the Gap started to form four hundred fifty million years ago when quartz pebbles were deposited in a shallow sea on top of the Ordovician Martinsburg shale. The Martinsburg shale was uplifted when a chain of volcanic islands collided with proto North America about four hundred fifty million years ago. These islands went over the North American plate. This collision deposited rock on top of this plate. Hence, this is how the Highlands and Kittatinny Valley were made.

Then about four hundred million years ago a small, long and thin continent collided with North America. Geologic pressure twisted the Silurian Shawangunk Conglomerate, therefore breaking the gray quartzite. Pressure from this continental strike, compressed the bed rock of the quartzite, made heat, allowed the quartzite to bend and melt silica to bond the quartz pebbles and other conglomerate together. Geologic pressure forced the quartzite up and the Delaware River slowly cut its way through the shattered quartzite. Otherwise the river may not have been able to cut its path.

Millions of years of ice, snow, rain, and wind erosion shaped the region. The Wisconsin Glacier that occurred between 21,000 BC to 13,000 BC covered Kittatinny Ridge and ended near Belvidere. This was the last touch to the Delaware Water Gap's look.

Regarding the geologic history of the Middle Delaware and how it relates to the Water Gap, the Central Delaware River cut a winding path out of solid rock and made a gap millions of years ago. Gradually the river eroded through conglomerate and sandstone rock belonging to the Blue Mountain range to create a visible gap, which is now the Delaware Water Gap.

The Blue Mountain range runs for 150 miles through Pennsylvania. The southwestern end of the mountain is at the Big Gap, west of Shippensburg, Penn. The northeastern end of the mountain is at the Delaware Water Gap on the New Jersey border. Mount Minsi creates the headland overseeing the Delaware River. The Blue Mountain Ridge continues northeast into New Jersey as the Kittatinny Mountains.

And although people can still see mountains along the main stem of the Delaware River in New Jersey and Pennsylvania, the main course of the Delaware has no waterfalls. However, since the 1880s, water tumbling over rocks and falling into foam has always attracted people to northeastern Pennsylvania. In fact, water today still cascades over the same rocks into the Delaware Water Gap National Recreation Area located near the Delaware Water Gap along the Appalachian Trail at Resort Point, Pennsylvania. Also the deformation of rock can be seen from the base of the Delaware Water Gap. The height of the Blue Mountains surrounding the Water Gap is approximately 1,200 feet.

Furthermore, the Delaware Water Gap National Recreation Area is an ideal example of a freshwater ecosystem. A riparian zone (river) borders this aquatic ecosystem forest buffer (a band of shrubs, trees, and native vegetation that borders a river or stream). The buffer zone protects the waterway by containing and filtering pollutants as the groundwater moves through the subsurface. Together, the river and buffer zone create the freshwater ecosystem.

As for its ecology, there are about 1,000 individually mapped wetlands in the Delaware Water Gap National Recreation Area. Big and small wetlands are intriguing places and all of these different wetlands play an important part in the ecology of the Delaware River Valley.

There are huge, complex forested wetland systems that begin on the top of the large ridges bordering the Delaware River, running downslope in a "braided drainage" pattern from terrace to terrace until they reach the broad river floodplain and wind their way to the Delaware River. There are broad expanses of marsh or wet meadow, characterized by sedges that look like grass but more frequently grow in thick tufts known as hummocks.

In addition, there are special wetlands like vernal pools and fens. Vernal pools are significant but often misunderstood wetlands. The typical vernal pool is a shallow depression on the forest floor that may or may not contain plants. A vernal pool normally holds water from about November to mid-June and is dry the rest of the year. It is the dry period that makes vernal pools so hard to identify as wetlands but so important.

Amphibians such as salamanders and wood frogs need pools of water to lay their eggs and let the tadpoles develop. The crucial factor is predators: if salamanders and frogs use ponds that contain fish, the fish typically eat the eggs and tadpoles, leaving so few that it can affect the whole population. Yet fortunately vernal pools dry up. That means they can't support fish, which means more eggs and tadpoles will survive.

Regarding fens, they are wetland communities that occur in areas where the underlying bedrock is limestone and therefore, very alkaline. Since most of the soils in the Delaware River Valley are acidic, plant communities that grow in fens are special and rather rare.

The Delaware Gap National Recreation Area also has many microclimates that sustain a wide variety of plant species ranging from aquatic plants to giant deciduous trees to cacti and ferns. Red maple, white oak and shagbark hickory are among the deciduous trees located in the hardwood forests while birch communities line streams and rivers. In addition, a large number of wildflowers like purple coneflower, wild bergamot, and yellow pond lily bloom during spring and summer and can be seen in all parts of the Recreation Area.

In regards to fishing, the Delaware Water Gap National Recreation Area has a variety of habitats for both cold-water and warm-water fish. The Recreation Area, which extends to both sides of the Delaware River in Pennsylvania and New York, is full of small ponds and lakes that provide panfish, great bass, and pickerel fishing. Brown and brook trout are also found in most streams, and an ideal brown drake hatch makes for prime fly-fishing. Furthermore, the central Delaware River gives anglers opportunities to catch muskellunge, American shad, walleye, smallmouth bass, and catfish.

Yet besides fishing opportunities that the Water Gap's Recreation Area offers to visitors and residents, the Middle Delaware overall is generally a clean river that is ideal for swimming, boating, kayaking, and canoeing.

Kayak trips are popular on the Delaware River through the Delaware Water Gap National Recreation Area in the scenic Pocono Mountains of northeastern Pennsylvania. The length of the trip ranges from a half day to numerous days of canoe camping adventures. The clear waters, with islands and beaches in the area, offer many opportunities for swimming, hiking and picnicking along the way. This path is geared toward novice and experienced kayakers. And fortunately for campers, Dingmans Campground, a 133-site rustic campground, is situated in the Pocono Mountains in Dingmans Ferry, Pennsylvania. Dingmans Campground, which is also part of the Delaware Water Gap National Recreational Area, provides a wide array of camp settings (including meadow and forest campsites), with its main sites located along the banks of the Delaware River.

As for the water in the Delaware Water Gap, it is typically fast flowing, smooth, and clear. There are a few small rapids, but the bulk of the river is a series of quiet pools and shallow riffles. The river substrate is cobbles and pebbles deposited by ancient glaciers. When it comes to water recreation, if you are looking for clean, easy-flowing, wide water with a lot of wildlife, the stretch of the Middle Delaware that runs through the Delaware Water Gap National Recreation Area from Milford to the Water Gap offers you an array of day and overnight adventures. Minisinks, then Namanock, are the first of a number of islands along this section of river, where the water starts to create pools.

Islands become markers for river sojourners through the National Recreation Area that had its origins from scuttled plans for Tocks, a dam at the island. The dam would have made the river over it a big reservoir. However, Tocks has remained along with Poxono, Depew, Sambo, and the rest, as stops by an easy ride spiced with egrets, wild turkey, heron, eagles, beaver, and bear.

Moreover, a lot of land in the Delaware Water Gap National Recreation Area lies within the floodplain of the Delaware River. In a floodplain, there is typically a high area along the riverbank between the primary stem of the river and low-lying areas that flood; it is the result of flooding and depositing of sediment over many years.

Over a period extending thousands of years, the chief stem of the river will gradually move back and forth between the two ridges that bound the floodplain. Regarding the Delaware River, the ridges are Pennsylvania's Pocono Plateau on the edge of the Appalachian Plateau on the west and on the east it's Kittatinny in New Jersey.

After floodplains accept water from a flooding river, they decrease the water flow force on the river's primary stem and prevent damage downstream. In addition, since water in a floodplain is not flowing it will deposit much of its sediment on the floodplain instead of transporting it downstream and depositing the sediment between bigger gravel and smooth cobble on the riverbed. This process is crucial for fish, which utilize the spaces between cobblestones as an area for depositing eggs, and to aquatic insects that hide and forage in these spaces.

In addition, included within Middle Delaware is Walpack Bend located downriver from Bushkill, Pa., with Flatbrookville, the closest New Jersey town. In this area, mountains and ridges on both sides embrace the Delaware making a quicker water flow and some sizable rapids. As you push off, the river appears straight and wide. However, even from here, looking downstream, you can see a mountain evidently blocking the way. At this region, the left bank of the Delaware is a ridge or frock. As you proceed, you're certain the river must disappear down a gigantic drain; it appears to go as straight as an arrow into the mountain in front.

Suddenly, the rock wall that was the left embankment of the river vanishes and the Delaware rushes through this breech, turning eastward and then northeastward, entirely reversing directions. It is at this breech that the Bushkill River enters on the right.

And it's no surprise that like the Upper Delaware River, the Middle Delaware has received *Wild and Scenic* designation through the National Wild and Scenic Rivers Act.

Delaware Water Gap that runs in between Pennsylvania and New Jersey.

The Delaware Water Gap slices through a huge ridge of the Appalachian Mountains.

Taken from the air, shooting down on the Delaware River by Randy Palmer, pilot and photographer.

Delaware Water Gap that runs in between Pennsylvania and New Jersey.

The Water Gap is a mile wide from Mount Tammany in New Jersey to Mount Minsi in Pennsylvania.

Taken from the air, shooting down on the Delaware River by Randy Palmer, pilot and photographer.

Delaware Water Gap that runs in between Pennsylvania and New Jersey.

The river through the Delaware Water Gap
is 283 feet above sea level.

*Taken from the air, shooting down on the Delaware River
by Randy Palmer, pilot and photographer.*

Delaware Water Gap that runs in between Pennsylvania and New Jersey.

The maximum depth of the Delaware River at the
Delaware Water Gap is about 55 feet.

*Taken from the air, shooting down on the Delaware River
by Randy Palmer, pilot and photographer.*

Delaware Water Gap that runs in between Pennsylvania and New Jersey.

Delaware Water Gap, which borders New Jersey and Pennsylvania, is an historic and scenic portion of the Middle Delaware River.

Taken from the air, shooting down on the Delaware River by Randy Palmer, pilot and photographer.

Lower Delaware
(Includes information on Penn's Landing and importance of habitat in river's urbanized section)

The Lower Delaware Estuary Region stretches south from the Delaware/Pennsylvania border to the point where the Delaware River opens to become the Delaware Bay. This area covers 1,020 square miles and is characterized by gently sloping topography in the north, giving way to flat coastal plain to the south. The region includes a patchwork landscape of forests and fields that are punctuated by development throughout, including Wilmington, Delaware. In regards to its economic impact to Delaware and Pennsylvania, riverfront industry and the Port of Wilmington make the Lower Estuary Region an important economic resource to both states.

As for the river itself, the Delaware originates in New York State and runs south into Pennsylvania, gaining strength from many tributaries along its path. This region east of the Appalachian Mountains is called the Piedmont Plateau and is characterized by rolling, upland hills and farmland.

The Delaware River then moves across the Piedmont Plateau, creating the border of Pennsylvania and New Jersey, and onto Morrisville, Pennsylvania where it meets the Coastal Plain. The Coastal Plain is flatter and made up of much sandier, softer soil without the rock content of the Piedmont.

Where two geological regions like this meet, it is known as the fall line. When a river crosses the fall line there is normally a huge change in its characteristics. Because Morrisville sits on the fall line between the Piedmont Plateau and the Coastal Plain, the Delaware River at the north end of town always flows downriver and is not affected by the tide. However, at Morrisville's south end, the Delaware has a huge tidal change and will change directions on a strong incoming tide.

This geological phenomenon that I just mentioned was crucial for early settlers for two reasons. First, this was as far up the river as a ship could go. The Delaware is more easily crossed upriver of the falls because it is narrower and shallower and bridges can be constructed easily for the same reasons. Second, there is typically a change in elevation making it possible to harness the power of the river to run the mills of colonial America.

But regardless of where the tide ends up at the fall line, the lower non-tidal Delaware River is the longest and busiest part of the river's three sections. The Lower Delaware River stretches almost 76 miles and begins just beneath the Delaware Water Gap in Warren County, Pennsylvania and ends at the tidal waters of the Delaware Bay near Trenton, New Jersey and Morrisville, Pennsylvania. The lower portion of the Delaware runs through the core of America's birthplace. Every turn in the river speaks to us of beauty, history, and opportunity.

As the Delaware River moves down past Trenton, New Jersey, freshwater starts to mix with saltwater from the Delaware Bay, making the Delaware Estuary, New Jersey's biggest estuary system. The Delaware Estuary provides an essential nursery environment for young fish to grow. Monitoring juvenile fish populations is necessary for fishery managers to estimate abundance and evaluate the viability of the population in New Jersey.

Yet in addition to the estuary's importance to New Jersey, from Philadelphia, Pennsylvania to New Castle, Delaware, the Lower Delaware River has been commercially successful for centuries, starting with its role as a distribution point for food grown inland. Furthermore, our country's history is found in the forests, farmland, canals, villages, inns, and mills along its way. Moreover, a variety of flora and fauna thrive on the Lower Delaware River's embankments and islands.

In regards to its geology and landforms, four geologic provinces in an east-west direction shape the Lower Delaware River corridor's varied landscapes. The topography of the northern end of the corridor is broken up by mountainous and rocky terrain. The middle river section is made up of rolling hills and clay soils. Finally, the southernmost province represents the flat, marshy, coastal plain.

In 2000, the Lower Delaware was designated a National Wild and Scenic River, which includes a 38.9-mile portion of the main stem Delaware connecting the Delaware Water Gap and Washington Crossing, Pennsylvania, just upstream of Trenton, New Jersey. Furthermore, three-quarters of the non-tidal Delaware River is now included in the national system.

The wetlands, streams, and floodplain, which are part of the Lower Delaware, define the river on the basis of its natural resources. The unique cliff formations overlooking the Lower Delaware combined with its islands, rapids, and other characteristics make this section of the Delaware River worthy of its *Wild and Scenic* designation. The Delaware River Basin Commission also recently classified the Lower Delaware as "Special Protection Water." This special protection status is a significant reminder that citizens can make a difference in protecting out waterways.

Furthermore, the Lower Delaware represents one of eight rivers in the National Parks Service's Partnership Rivers Program. The special feature of "Partnership Rivers" is that they flow mainly through private property. Flowing mainly through private land means that local municipalities (33 along the Lower Delaware in Pennsylvania and New Jersey), not the federal government, play the role in managing these significant natural resources.

Regarding mammals that inhabit the Lower Delaware, river otter, beaver, white-tailed deer, and four bat species (small-footed, Northern long-eared, Keen's and Indiana) are commonly found in Hunterdon County, New Jersey and upper Bucks County, Pennsylvania.

In addition to mammals, fish, specifically sturgeons, can be seen in the Lower Delaware. The shortnose sturgeon can be found in the lower portion of the Delaware between Philadelphia, Pa. and Trenton, New Jersey, whereas Atlantic sturgeon swims as far upriver as Trenton. The Lower Delaware also hosts a tremendous smallmouth bass fishery that is an ideal area for anglers engaging in fly and light tackle sport fishing. Besides finfish, downriver at Tohickon Creek, Pennsylvania is where you can find a stream of high water quality where rare species (freshwater sponges and mussels) grow.

Besides fish and other wildlife, plants make up a crucial part of the Lower Delaware's ecosystem. Cliffs as high as 400 feet above the valley floor provide a desert-like environment for the eastern red cedar. In Hunterdon, New Jersey, Prickly Pear can be found, as well as Green Violet and Smooth Veiny Peavine.

Rare northeastern U.S. Roseroot, an arctic-alpine herb, grows on shelves and in crevices at Nockamixon Cliffs in

Pennsylvania. Meanwhile, rare species such as riverweed grow in Tohickon Creek, Pa.

Within the river corridor's floodplain, lush areas of willow, spirea, silk dogwood and alder shrubs can be found. The riverside vegetation varies with the geology and soils in the river corridor. This vegetation also provides crucial habitat for mammals, birds, and shades the water for fish.

This part of the river also offers people many recreational opportunities. Here is where visitors can engage in boating, canoeing, kayaking, and tubing. Also guests with fishing licenses can fish for shad, striped bass, walleye pike, muskellunge, and other fish. In addition, during the spring and summer many blueback herring migrate to the Lower Delaware to reproduce.

The Lower Delaware River serves as a water transportation route for Philadelphia, Pennsylvania, Trenton and Camden, New Jersey and Wilmington, Delaware, all of which help create one of our country's great, important, industrial regions. The Lower Delaware is the section of the waterway that is the primary shipping route where it is navigable by huge, oceangoing ships as far inland as Philadelphia, Pa. and by smaller vessels to Trenton, New Jersey.

Above Trenton, New Jersey, the river becomes shallow and rock infested, so most of the bigger boats run south of there. Due to the commercial shipping interests, the Delaware has a dredged channel that is normally in the forty-foot depth range.

Regarding Philadelphia and large ships, Penn's Landing on the Lower Delaware comes to mind. The Penn's Landing Area stretches along the Delaware River for about ten blocks from Vine Street to South Street and encompasses the spot where William Penn, Philadelphia's founder, first touched ground. After Penn's arrival, this area soon became the center of Philly's maritime soul and the city's main commercial district.

Penn's Landing Marina is home to the *Becuna* submarine and to the *Olympia* warship cruiser. The marina is also available to private boaters. Today, Penn's Landing is one of the world's biggest freshwater ports and is now a 37-acre-long riverside park, the site of concerts and summer festivals where Philadelphians and tourists meet for entertainment. In addition, on December 31, residents of Philadelphia gather at the landing to usher in the New Year. There is also the cyberwalk down Penn's Landing that begins by heading over the Market Street Bridge onto the Landing. From the bridge, you look across the river into Camden, New Jersey where you will see a tower attached to an old factory.

Penn's Landing is also home to the Independence Seaport Museum and a flotilla of ship museums. The ship museums include the *USS Olympia*, the *USS Becuna*, the *Gazela* of Philadelphia, and tugboat *Jupiter*.

The Independence Seaport Museum celebrates Philadelphia's maritime history and is a waterfront cultural and educational center. The museum explores Philadelphia's waterfront and its impact on our entire nation. The centerpiece exhibit is called "Home Port: Philadelphia" that dives into twelve different waterfront worlds that include naval defense, commerce and trade and shipbuilding.

Also displayed throughout the museum are nautical relics such as a champagne bottle encased in silver that was used to christen the *USS Philadelphia*. In addition, the museum showcases products brought into Philadelphia, shipbuilding tools, and artwork.

The *USS Olympia*, now a ship museum, was constructed in 1892 and was one of America's first steel ships. This historic battleship became the flagship of the North Atlantic Squadron and protected U.S. interests in many foreign countries. During World War I, the *Olympia* served as an escort ship to the Atlantic Ocean. Its last assignment, in 1921, was transporting the body of the Unknown Soldier back from Europe and carrying him to his final resting-place at Arlington National Cemetery in Virginia.

Besides the *USS Olympia*, there is the *USS Becuna* that was a submarine used during World War II; the *Becuna* was commissioned in 1944 to serve as the submarine flagship of the Southwest Pacific Fleet under General Douglas MacArthur. This sub was credited with destroying thousands of tons of Japanese merchant and naval ships including a battleship.

After the war, the *Becuna* was re-equipped with a larger electric battery, sophisticated radar, and torpedoes with nuclear warheads. The submarine went on to serve in the Atlantic and Mediterranean during the Korean and Vietnam Wars. Finally, the *Becuna* became a training submarine at New London, Connecticut and was decommissioned in 1969.

The *Gazela* of Philadelphia is another historic ship that was constructed in 1883. This vessel was originally a Portuguese fishing boat and during the 1960s was seeking cod in Canadian waters.

Later in 1969, the Philadelphia Ship Preservation Guild acquired the ship. The Guild is an organization that maintains and operates the 177-foot-long vessel that now functions as a floating classroom for people interested in learning nautical terminology, knot-tying, and maritime matters. Today, the *Gazela* is still seaworthy and sets sail each year to visit ports of the world. The *Gazela* was also the oldest tall ship to participate in the OpSail Tall Ship Festival in 1976. In 1986, the ship took part in the Statue of Liberty's 100th birthday celebration in New York Harbor.

Moreover, Penn's Landing is where people can board the *Spirit of Philadelphia*, a riverboat and sightseeing cruise ship that docks alongside Columbus Blvd. at Penn's Landing next to the Chart House Restaurant. Before departure from the upper deck of the *Spirit*, visitors can look north toward the Ben Franklin Bridge and get a good view of the overall Lower Delaware River Area.

The *Spirit of Philadelphia* entertains tourists and local residents with scenic lunch and dinner cruises on the Delaware River. The ship features three enclosed decks that hold up to 550 passengers in cruise-style seating. In addition, a fourth deck offers outdoor patio-style seating for those who want to dine alfresco as they experience the unique sights of the Delaware River shoreline, including the *Battleship New Jersey*, the New Jersey State Aquarium, and the Philadelphia Naval Base.

Along with Penn's Landing, Camden, New Jersey, located only one mile from Philadelphia's historic district, is a popular waterfront area on the Lower Delaware.

One interesting, historic attraction the Camden Waterfront offers that you won't want to miss is the *Battleship New Jersey*. Today, our nation's most decorated battleship is the area's most interesting museum, open for public tours and events. Exploring the *USS New Jersey* (BB62) is experiencing history in a new way. Besides looking at artifact exhibits from the ship's past, you can tour the entire ship.

Historically speaking, the BB62 was built at the Philadelphia Naval Shipyard and launched on December 7, 1942; just a year after the Pearl Harbor attack brought the U.S. into

World War II. The *USS New Jersey* was the second U.S. Navy ship to be called "New Jersey," the first being BB16, a turn of the century (19th-century battleship).

The BB62 was decommissioned for the last time on February 8, 1991 at Bremerton, Washington where she resided until she returned home to New Jersey. On November 11, 1999, the *New Jersey* returned to the Philadelphia Naval Shipyard. Since that period, she has been restored, opened, and established as an educational museum and tribute to soldiers that served our country. Then in October 2001, the *Battleship New Jersey* opened as a museum and memorial.

In addition to Penn's Landing, the Delaware Canal represents the history of the Lower Delaware. The canal, built in the mid-19th century, stretches from Bristol to Easton, Pa. along the Delaware River. It was used to haul coal and other products from the Lehigh Canal in Pennsylvania to the industrial centers of the Philadelphia area near Bristol, Pa. The canal ran its last commercial traffic in October 1931. The state of Pennsylvania purchased forty miles of the canal in 1931 and bought the remaining twenty miles in 1940.

Yet it wasn't only the Delaware Canal that was important for river transportation in the Lower Delaware hundreds of years ago, ferries were also significant. In fact, two ferries that crossed the river in the Trenton, New Jersey area date from the late 17th century – the Yardley Ferry and the Trenton or Middle Ferry. Two more ferries (the Upper and Lower Ferries) were added later in the 18th century.

The Yardley Ferry was established in 1683, formalized through an act of the Pennsylvania Assembly in 1722 and operated until the mid-1830s.

The Trenton or Middle Ferry, which may have been in place as early as 1675, crossed the Delaware from Ferry Street in Trenton and the Pennsylvania Assembly authorized this ferry in 1718.

On the Pennsylvania side of the Delaware River, the rights to the Trenton Ferry passed between the Biles, Chorley and Kirkbridge families prior to being bought by Patrick Colvin in 1772. In New Jersey, during the Colonial Period, owners of the property known today as the William Trent House controlled the ferry. The patent of 1726 guaranteed James Trent, William's son, exclusive ferry rights along the New Jersey riverbank.

In the 1750s, one operator, Andrew Ramsay, linked the Trenton Ferry to the stagecoach line between Trenton and New Brunswick, New Jersey and a downriver boat service in Philadelphia, Pa. During the 1770s, as Lamberton, New Jersey, a fishing village, transformed into a river town and Trenton's port, a second trans-Delaware ferry was added. Set up by Elijah Bond in New Jersey and John Thornton in Pennsylvania in 1773, this ferry was known as the Lamberton or Lower Ferry.

For many years, the Lamberton Ferry competed with the Trenton Ferry, serving between 1776 and 1781 as the "continental ferry" where Americans that actively served in the military could cross the Delaware at reduced rates. During the Revolutionary War Period, a third ferry called the Upper Ferry began operating. Crossing close to where the Calhoun Street Bridge (connects Trenton, New Jersey with Morrisville, Pa.) spans the Delaware today, this ferry was used around the time of the Battles of Trenton in the winter of 1776-77. All three Trenton ferries (Upper, Middle and Lower) competed for river crossing business for about 25 years or so. However, after the first bridge that joined Trenton, New Jersey with Morrisville, Pa. was opened in 1806, the importance of ferries faded rapidly.

In regards to ferry facilities, most ferryboats were either of raft-like pontoon construction or long, narrow, flat-bottomed vessels with low sides and hinged flaps at each end to facilitate unloading and loading. Oars, poles and sometimes sails were used to help navigate the river currents and other items like ropes, chains, and hooks that were part of the ferryman's equipment. The ferry terminus frequently emerged as the hub of a bigger settlement that consisted of a ferry house, a tavern and other residences. For example, during the mid-18th century, the Trenton Ferry was a small but lively riverside enclave.

Overall, the Lower Delaware as a whole has a history of its own apart from the rest of the river as it runs between two colonial cities of our country: New York and Philadelphia. National historic districts and sites are along the lower river and at Washington Crossing, Pennsylvania, you too, can "cross the Delaware" just like General George Washington did (from Pennsylvania to Trenton, New Jersey) during the late 1700s.

In addition to its rich history, it might be hard to imagine a place for wildlife along the lower, urbanized section of the Delaware River. I am specifically referring to Philadelphia, Pa., Trenton and Camden, New Jersey and Wilmington, Delaware with its big industry, power plants, oil refineries, highways, railroads, bridges, dikes, and parking lots. The closest many people get to the waterfront is crossing over one of its many bridges. But habitat is crucial even in urban environments.

Maintaining a natural environment along a riverfront is equally important to the Delaware's urban portion. Natural habitat prevents erosion and flooding, improves water quality, supports fish and wildlife that depend on the river, and enhances recreational activities and tourism. For many years, habitat restoration along the urban corridor of the Delaware and near the mouths of tributaries has been ignored. Restoration projects have focused more in the less developed lower reaches of the Delaware River. Pollutants from urban run-off, contaminated sites, dredging, fill projects, and spills continually stress what little habitat does exist in the densely populated portion of the Delaware.

Habitat loss in the Lower Delaware has severely impacted many species. Pollution has resulted in fishing restrictions and advisories, and stigmatized people's opinion of the Delaware River. Public access to the waterfront has also been restricted. Furthermore, both development and pollution increases flooding and impacts the cultural, human, economic and natural functions of riverfront communities.

But habitat restoration efforts can increase the economic return on revitalization efforts of the regional and site-specific level, as well as provide significant habitat linkages throughout the Delaware Estuary. The cleanup and revitalization of contaminated sites offers a prime opportunity for people and wildlife to return to the Lower Delaware Riverfront. Habitat restoration can easily be included in redevelopment projects.

Scientists and environmentalists have stated that the best ways to restore the river are to address barriers to natural functioning, such as dikes, dams, ditches, and other man-made structures and allow natural drainage and hydrology patterns to reestablish themselves. Restoration in the lower end of the river is important as it increases recreational opportunities, offers important habitat linkages, and improves water quality and flood control.

A good example of waterfront revitalization is the Peterson Wildlife Refuge in Wilmington, Delaware. More than 230 acres have been restored in a previously ditched and diked marsh by reestablishing natural tidal inundations, restoring stream channels, and lowering the marsh elevation in certain areas. The urban wildlife refuge along Wilmington's waterfront provides access to wildlife recreation and educates the city's residents and schoolchildren.

Riverfront habitat restoration in the Lower Delaware also provides important economic benefits. For instance, a cost benefit analysis of alternative greenway scenarios along the North Delaware Riverfront in Philadelphia determined that annual public benefits associated with an alternative providing ecological restoration generate the biggest net benefit to the city and highest annual percent return on public investment with an estimated $2.5 billion impact on the local economy.

Together with its habitat restoration, boating, other recreational opportunities, history, geology, wildlife, quaint historic towns with unique landscape on the New Jersey, Pennsylvania and Delaware sides of the river, and its importance as a "working waterway," the Lower Delaware has become an important and interesting portion of the Delaware River to see by both local residents and tourists.

Lower Delaware River at Penn's Landing in Philadelphia, Pa.

Taken from the air, shooting down on the Delaware River by Randy Palmer, pilot and photographer.

Lower Delaware River at Penn's Landing in Philadelphia, Pa.

Taken from the air, shooting down on the Delaware River by Randy Palmer, pilot and photographer.

Lower Delaware River at Penn's Landing in Philadelphia, Pa.

Taken from the air, shooting down on the Delaware River by Randy Palmer, pilot and photographer.

Lower Delaware River at Penn's Landing in Philadelphia, Pa.

Taken from the air, shooting down on the Delaware River by Randy Palmer, pilot and photographer.

Lower Delaware River at Penn's Landing in Philadelphia, Pa.

Taken from the air, shooting down on the Delaware River by Randy Palmer, pilot and photographer.

Delaware Valley, Kittatinny Mountain Region and Delaware River Highlands

The Delaware Valley is a name referring to the metropolitan area centered on the City of Philadelphia, Pa. The name is evolved from the Delaware River that passes through the region, although the river stretches over a hundred miles north of Philadelphia. The Valley is made up of several counties in southeastern Pennsylvania and southern New Jersey, one relatively populated county in northern Delaware and one small county in northeastern Maryland. Philadelphia, being the area's main commercial, industrial, and cultural center, has a big sphere of influence that affects those counties surrounding it. So to no surprise, most of the region's population resides in Pennsylvania and New Jersey.

Yet despite Philadelphia's gigantic presence and influence in the area, the character of the Delaware Valley is also made up of suburbs. King of Prussia, Pennsylvania and Cherry Hill Township, New Jersey, are two of the biggest suburban edge cities. The suburbs of Philadelphia consist of a huge concentration of malls, including the King of Prussia Mall in Pennsylvania (biggest on the East Coast) and the Cherry Hill Mall in Cherry Hill Township, New Jersey (first enclosed mall on the East Coast). Malls, shopping centers, offices, highways, and houses continue to replace rolling rural areas, farmlands, forests, and wetlands.

However, due to recent opposition by politicians and residents, many acres of property have been preserved throughout the Delaware Valley. Straggling woodlands and farmlands can still be seen throughout the area, providing a haven for nature seekers. In Pennsylvania, older and smaller towns and big boroughs like Norristown, Jenkintown, and West Chester, all kept their unique community identities despite being bombarded in suburbia.

Moreover, the Delaware Valley has a huge and growing ethnic population due to job growth and its proximity to major cities outside of Philadelphia, like New York City (90 miles away) and Washington, DC (140 miles away).

Counties that make up the Valley include New Castle County in Delaware and Cecil County in Maryland. In Pennsylvania, you will find Berks County, Bucks County, Chester

County, Delaware County, Montgomery County, and Philadelphia County. Across the Delaware River in New Jersey, the Valley's counties include Burlington County, Camden County, Cumberland County (Vineland Metropolitan Region), Gloucester County, and Salem County.

The Delaware Valley also consists of Atlantic County and Cape May County in New Jersey. These two counties are home to Philadelphia commuters along with a huge tourism industry.

In addition, Ocean County, New Jersey, while designated as part of the New York Metropolitan Area, is strongly associated with the Valley. In fact, Ocean County has many tourist attractions often visited by residents of the Delaware Valley. These attractions include beaches like Long Beach Island and Seaside Heights, along with resorts such as Six Flags Great Adventure. Moreover, the Jersey Shore is a big destination for beach tourism for residents of Delaware Valley.

Besides counties in New Jersey, major cities in the Delaware Valley include Camden and Vineland. In Pennsylvania, the cities are Chester, Reading, and Philadelphia. In Delaware, the Valley's main city is located in Wilmington.

Western New Jersey and eastern Pennsylvania are where the Delaware River Valley and Ridge Region is located. This region is a continuation of the overall stratigraphy and structure of the Hudson Valley and Catskills Region with some noticeable exceptions. The main sediment source areas during the Taconic and Acadian Orogenies were to the northeast in the New England Region. Thus the coarse caustic units grow progressively thinner and finer grained. In contrast, the marine mudrocks and carbonate units typically grow thicker toward the southeast where shallow inland seas invaded the Appalachian Basin Area for longer periods of time.

North and west of Kittatinny Mountain the great folds of the Valley and Ridge constantly flatten out. North of the New York/Pennsylvania border, the structural deformation is limited to a series of gentle, broad synclines and anticlines.

Heading southward, the Port Jervis Trough Valley is between Port Jervis, New York and Stroudsburg, Pennsylvania where the Delaware River follows the strike of Lower and Middle Devonian strata. The rocks are steeply dipping toward the west. To the east, the Silurian Shawangunk Formation creates the crest of

Kittatinny Mountain, and to the west, the Late Devonian Catskill Group forms the erosionally dissected plateau of the Pocono Mountains in Pennsylvania.

A lot of the Delaware River Valley and Kittatinny Ridge in New Jersey encompass part of the Delaware Water Gap National Recreation Area. The Kittatinny Mountains are an extension of the Ridge and Valley Province of the Appalachian Mountains that stretch from near the Hudson River in New York to South Central Pennsylvania. Looking west of the Ridge is known as the Allegheny Plateau, and looking east from the Ridge is the "Great Valley."

The Delaware Valley also attracts many birds to the area. As part of the Atlantic flyway, the corridor is home to a huge number of water birds and waterfowl in the wooded riverside habitats.

There are also many species of butterflies in the Delaware River Valley, but the Monarch is one of the most popular butterflies. Each summer, monarchs arrive from Mexico after wintering there during our coldest months.

The Delaware River is older than the present mountains along it, having cut water gaps that are perpendicular to hard strata ridges. The Delaware River that forms Pennsylvania's eastern border with New Jersey slices through the Kittatinny Ridge just southeast of Stroudsburg, Pennsylvania. The Delaware Valley also has a very long cultural history; native Americans first settled here at about 8000 BC.

In addition to the Delaware Valley, there is the Delaware River Highlands, an area located on each side of the Upper Delaware River Valley. The Highlands encompassing parts of three states and five counties: Pike and Wayne Counties in Pennsylvania, Sullivan and Orange in New York and Sussex in New Jersey.

Named, literally, for the "high land" on either side of the Delaware River, the region is densely forested and features many waterfalls, as every stream flowing into the Delaware River must cut through the escarpment on either side of the river. Numerous large parcels of state and federal property, including two large National Park Service properties, the 69,000 acre Delaware Water Gap National Recreation Area and the 75,000 acre Upper Delaware Scenic and Recreational River.

A wide array of outdoor recreational activities including bird watching, fishing, hunting, and hiking draw visitors from all over the world to this river valley. In fact, now the Delaware River Highlands is one of the biggest bald eagle wintering grounds in North America. Hundreds of eagles return here each winter for the undisturbed habitat, open water and ample fish populations that they need in order to survive winter. Eagles mate for life and return to the same general areas from which they fledged. Nests are reused and added to each year; becoming eight or more feet deep, six feet wide and weighing hundreds of pounds. Moreover, although eagles can be seen in the Delaware River Highlands Region year-round, mid-December through February are the best months for viewing.

As for fishing, Delaware River Highlands offers thousands of places to fish for species such as trout, walleye, bass, and American shad. Fishing licenses, available at many sporting goods stores and some town halls, are required for anglers 16 and older. An additional permit is required for trout.

Trout are plentiful in most of the rapid-flowing cold streams and rivers in the region, including the Delaware and Lackawaxen Rivers. Smallmouth bass can be found in both rivers and in large streams. Striped bass and American shad are found mostly in the Delaware River. In addition, there are many boat accesses to the Delaware River and most are free. Please note that not every ramp is suitable for every craft, as not every body of water is suitable for every craft.

The region also offers excellent hunting for black bear, white-tailed deer, and wild turkey, as well as some of the state's best waterfowl, snowshoe hare and ruffed grouse hunting. Hunters need to pay close attention to each state's hunting regulations and acquire the appropriate licenses and designated permits.

Hiking is another popular recreational activity on the Appalachian National Scenic Trail. This public trail is 2,155 miles-long and 60 of its miles follow the Kittatinny Ridge in New Jersey (found in the Appalachian Ridge and Valley Region of New Jersey) to near the Lehigh Gap in Pa. to and through the Delaware Water Gap. You can also hike on the Delaware Water Gap Trails. The Water Gap has sixty hiking trails (25 miles make up the Appalachian Trail) and there are six trails close to the Pocono

Environmental Education Center in Pa. ranging from a quarter mile to five miles.

Some Tributaries (includes the main ones) and Main Reservoirs of the Delaware River

Significant tributaries of the Delaware River include the Neversink River, Mongaup River, and Callicoon Creek in New York; the Lehigh, Schuylkill, and Lackawaxen rivers in Pennsylvania, the Musconetcong and Maurice rivers in New Jersey, and the Christina River in Delaware that flows through parts of Pennsylvania and Maryland.

Located in southeastern New York, the Neversink River is the longest tributary of the Delaware River in New York State. The river's name, Neversink, which is about 65 miles long, derives from an Algonquian language phrase meaning "mad river." The Neversink originates just south of the border between Ulster and Sullivan counties, where its west and east branches join near the hamlet of Claryville. Both branches start on the slopes of Slide Mountain, which is the tallest peak in the Catskills.

Although most of the property around it is privately owned, the Neversink in its upper section is a wild and rocky stream ideal for trout fishing. In fact, many consider the Neversink River to be the birthplace of American dry fly fishing. Besides trout, the river is home to other fish species that include American eel, sucker, bluegill, carp, and smallmouth bass. In addition to fish, the river has a variety of flora and fauna. While fishing is the main recreational activity on the Neversink, some swimming holes are available along with limited boating.

Not far downstream from the confluence in Neversink, it is impounded to create the Neversink Reservoir, which is located in Sullivan County's Town of Neversink. A five-mile water tunnel to Rondout Reservoir, and subsequently to the Delaware Aqueduct connects the Neversink River. The Neversink Reservoir was made by the displacement of many locals, as many towns along the river were flooded, which created the reservoir. Generally, the reservoir flows southeasterly through the Catskill Mountains and is impounded in the town of Neversink to form the Neversink Reservoir of the New York City Water Supply System. In addition to New York City, the reservoir provides water to other communities along its water supply network.

In addition to the Neversink Reservoir is the Neversink Gorge. The Gorge is located in Forestburgh, New York and is one of the most spectacular features of the Neversink River. A portion of the western side of the Gorge (above Denton Falls through High Falls to the entrance of Eden Brook) is a private nature sanctuary called The Turner Brook Reserve. The eastern side and the rest of the western property are a New York State Department of Environmental Conservation Region often called the Neversink Gorge Unique Area.

Digressing to the river, it is located about two hours from New York City, The Neversink River Watershed provides habitat for more than 30 rare species and natural communities. It is an ecological jewel with rushing waters, which host a spectacular and diverse array of life.

Along this river lies the 550-acre Neversink River Preserve in Orange County, New York where the world's healthiest population of globally endangered dwarf wedgemussel thrives. In addition to wedgemussel, the preserve provides habitat for a variety of trees, wildflowers, fish, birds, reptiles, amphibians, and mammals.

Trees grown at the Neversink River Preserve include red and sugar maples, sycamores, river birch, red oaks and green ash. Wildflowers are Dutchman's breeches, closed gentians, cardinal flowers, bee balm, blue flags, trout lilies and violets.

In addition, there are 40 species of fish found in the preserve. Some fish found there include the sea lamprey, brook trout, American shad and American eel. Along with fish, birds spotted there consist of northern harriers, owls, bald eagles, ruffed grouse, belted kingfishers, osprey, common mergansers, blue herons, wood ducks, and many warblers and songbirds.

Reptiles inhabiting the preserve are snapping turtles, ribbon snakes, and northern water snakes. Joining the reptiles are amphibians (wood frogs and spotted salamanders). Finally, mammals, which include beaver and otter, live in the creeks and wetlands that cross the reservation. Meanwhile, wild turkeys, bobcats, and black bear inhabit the forests and meadows.

Moving on to another Delaware tributary named the Mongaup River; this river enters the Delaware River about six miles north of Port Jervis, New York. A portion of Mongaup that flows 2.9 miles by Sullivan and Orange counties in New York is best known for its nature scenery and water activities. During the summer, this part of the Mongaup provides whitewater for rafters, paddlers, and kayakers. The only paddling stretch along Mongaup River is from Rio Dam to the Delaware River. Hiking is another popular thing for people to do along the Mongaup.

A major tributary of Mongaup River is the Middle Mongaup River, which is well known for American Bald Eagle watching. This area by Middle Mongaup also provides one of the biggest concentrations of wintering bald eagles in New York State.

Besides eagles, the Mongaup River Valley is a bird conservation area where people can see Cerulean Warbler and Red-Shouldered Hawk (both are special concern species). Moreover, the gigantic forest of Mongaup's Watershed supports significant habitat, including rare species like a perched bog, a flood plain forest, and pitch pine-oak-heath woodland. Spotted salamander and timber rattlesnake have also been documented there.

New York State is also home to Callicoon Creek, a Delaware tributary in Sullivan County. This creek is well known for its ten mile-long East Branch that supplies whitewater for adventurous people who enjoy river kayaking, paddling, or rafting during the summer.

Another main Delaware tributary is the Lehigh River, a 103-mile long river that runs in eastern Pennsylvania. The Lehigh circulates in a winding course through valleys between ridges of the Appalachian Mountains. Its upper course is comprised of many whitewater rapids that provide the means for whitewater kayaking, canoeing, and rafting. Its lower course creates the core of the Lehigh Valley, a historically significant anthracite coal and steel-producing region of Pennsylvania.

The Lehigh River rises in the Pocono Mountains of northeastern Pennsylvania and it initially moves southwest, through southern Lackawanna County. Near White Haven, it turns south following a zigzag whitewater course through Lehigh Gorge State Park then southeast past Lehighton. Southeast of Lehighton, it passes through Blue Mountain in a narrow opening called the Lehigh Gap.

Finally, from the Lehigh Gap, the Lehigh River flows southeast to Allentown, Pa. where it is joined by the Little Lehigh Creek, and then northeast past Bethlehem, where it joins the

Delaware River in Easton Pa., along Pennsylvania's boundary with New Jersey.

In addition to Lehigh, the 130-mile-long Schuylkill River flows in Pennsylvania and its watershed lies entirely within the state. The river winds through Philadelphia as it passes popular structures and facilities that include 30th Street Station, the Schuylkill Expressway, Amtrak train tracks creating part of the Northeast corridor, the Spring Garden Ave. Bridge, Boathouse Row and the Philadelphia Museum of Art. The Schuylkill pronounced ("SKOO-kull"), joins the Delaware River, of which it is the largest tributary, at the Philadelphia Naval Business Center, just northeast of Philadelphia International Airport.

The Delaware Indians were the first settlers of the region around the Schuylkill River, which they called Ganshohawanee, meaning, "roaring and rushing waters." Its European founder, Arendt Corssen of the Dutch West India Company, later gave the river the name Schuylkill.

The Schuylkill is a designated Pennsylvania Scenic River and its watershed of about 2,000 square miles lies totally within the state of Pennsylvania. Its eastern branch is in the Appalachian Mountains at Tuscarora Springs, near Tamaqua in Schuylkill County. The western branch begins near Minersville and it joins the eastern branch at Schuylkill Haven.

Regarding recreation, the Schuylkill River is now well known with water sports enthusiasts. The Dad Vail Regatta, a yearly rowing competition, is organized on the river near Boathouse Row along with the annual Bayada Regatta, featuring disabled rowers from all over the nation.

Finally, there's the Lackawaxen River in northeastern Pennsylvania. The Lackawaxen, which is about 25 miles long, flows through a huge countryside area in the northern Pocono Mountains, draining an area of about 598 square miles.

The West Branch Lackawaxen River is about fifteen miles long. It ascends in northern Wayne County, Pa. and runs south, southeast. After its confluence with Johnson Creek, the main stream flows southeast through Prompton Lake reservoir where it is joined from the southwest by Wallenpaupack Creek. The West Brach continues east and meets the Delaware River at Lackawaxen.

Lackawaxen River's source is in western Wayne County about five miles northeast of Forest City. This river is a well-known destination for recreational fly fishing for trout and canoeing.

In New Jersey, there's the forty-four-mile-long Musconetcong River (another Delaware tributary) that runs through the rural mountainous terrain of northwestern Jersey. The Musconetcong moves through Lake Musconetcong, then flows southwest past Stephensburg and New Hampton, passing south of Washington then by the southeastern part of the Pohatcong Mountain ridge. This tributary then meets the Delaware River across from Riegelsville, Pennsylvania. The river does not pass through any big population center and has been the site of little industrial development throughout its history.

The second important tributary of the Delaware River in southwestern New Jersey is the 50-mile-long Maurice River. The Maurice River, pronounced "Morris," is the second largest and longest tributary to Delaware Bay. Its watershed consists of a broad southern portion of forested wetlands known as Pine Barrens. This river's mouth on Delaware Bay is surrounded by big saltmarshes and it provides a historically significant ground for oysters.

The river forms an important ecological link between the Pine Barrens and the Delaware Bay Systems. It is located in the only stand of wild rice in New Jersey and provides habitat for 53 percent of the species in New Jersey designated as endangered. In 1993, Congress designated 28.9 miles of the Maurice River and its tributaries as the Maurice National Scenic and Recreational River.

Yet another significant tributary of the Delaware River is the Christina River. This 35-mile-long river runs in northern Delaware and also flows through small areas of southeastern Pennsylvania and northeastern Maryland. Close to its mouth the river moves past downtown Wilmington, Del., creating the city's harbor for traffic on the Delaware River. As for its recreational use, many rowing teams and clubs in Wilmington now practice along the Christina River.

The Christina River rises in southeastern Pennsylvania in Chester County, and initially flows southeastwardly, proceeding through northeastern Cecil County, Maryland into New Castle County in Delaware where it gushes through southern and western areas of Newark, Del. Then it turns northeastwardly, passing the town of Newport and approaching Wilmington from the southwest. The Christina River receives White Clay Creek from the west and Brandywine Creek in Wilmington about two miles upstream of its mouth.

The Christina River and its tributaries drain an area of 565 square miles. About 71% of the Christina's basin is located in Pennsylvania, 28 percent is in Delaware, and 1 percent is in Maryland. The basin's streams provide about 100 million gallons of water per day for over a half a million people in the three states, providing 75% of the water supply for New Castle County, Delaware, and over 40% of the water supply for Chester County, Pennsylvania.

The river was named for Queen Christina of Sweden. In 1638, the original permanent European settlement in Delaware was established at the confluence of Brandywine Creek and the Christina River as part of the Swedish colony of New Sweden.

As I mentioned earlier, Brandywine Creek, also called Brandywine River, flows through Wilmington, Delaware and Chester County, Pa. It is also near the Christina River as it branches off the Delaware River. Brandywine Creek is winding and narrow and can be muddy or shallow, depending on the season. Brandywine is actually a creek and has been important to the development of the area.

In Chester County, Pennsylvania during the American Revolution, the Battle of Brandywine Creek took place on September 11, 1777 when George Washington was in charge of the American troops. America lost the Battle of Brandywine but it was still an important battle during the Revolutionary War.

Before the Revolutionary War, the Lenni Lenape Indians lived on the banks of Brandywine Creek because of the access to the water and the nature around it, including hunting, fishing, and growing crops. The Indians had three main tribes (the Munsee, the Unalchigo, and the Unami). While the Lenni Lenape Indians lived on the bank of the Brandywine, English settlers were moving into Chester County.

Outside of Chester County, Pennsylvania, there is yet another important Delaware River tributary in Bucks County, Pa which is named, Tinicum Creek.

Tinicum Creek is a waterway of exceptional value that drains the townships of Nockamixon and Tinicum in Upper Bucks County, Pennsylvania. With its two main branches, Rapp and Beaver Run Creeks, the Tinicum is a named tributary included in the designation of the Lower Delaware National Wild and Scenic River. Descending almost 500 feet from the headwaters of its two branches, the stream enters the Delaware River south of Erwinna, Pa. and north of Point Pleasant, Pa., running under State Route 32 (River Road) and the Delaware Canal. The Tinicum is also a 36 square-mile watershed laced with almost forty miles of named and unnamed streams.

Before Europeans settled in the Tinicum Creek Watershed, it was inhabited by the Lenni Lenape Indian tribe, many of who later intermarried with Irish and German settlers and whose families remain in the region today. A lot of names of places in the watershed are Lenape in origin, including "Tinicum," which means "along the edge of the island."

In 1999, a study conducted in Bucks County, Pennsylvania ranked the entire Tinicum Creek Watershed as first priority to protect. This study was based on the watershed's variety of uncommon plant communities, numerous rare plant and animal species, and the exceptional quality of the water. Over 100 nesting bird species and 400 plant species inhabit the watershed.

Two other Delaware River tributaries in Pennsylvania consist of Tohickon Creek and Ridley Creek.

Tohickon Creek is the longest waterway located entirely in Bucks County, Pa. The creek starts its journey in Springfield Township and has its confluence with the Delaware River at Point Pleasant, Pennsylvania. Tohickon Creek is dammed to create the popular Lake Nockamixon.

Ridley Creek is located in southwest Pennsylvania. Two branches of Ridley Creek rise between Malvern and Frazer in Chester County, Pa. and then join about a mile south in Frazer. The creek then runs south then southeast to enter Delaware County and Ridley State Park. After it leaves the park, it passes the town of Media, Pa. while entering a deep gorge. Before flowing into the Delaware River, Ridley Creek creates the border of Chester and the borough of Eddystone, both communities situated in Pennsylvania.

Other Delaware River tributaries in New Jersey include the Salem River, Alloway Creek, Assunpink Creek, Cooper River, Crosswicks Creek, and Paulins Kill.

The Salem River is a 34.7-mile-long tributary of the Delaware River in southwestern New Jersey. The watershed and course of the Salem River are completely within Salem County. The river rises in Upper Pittsgrove Township and moves initially westward, through the borough of Woodstown and along the boundaries of Mannington Townships and Carneys Point. Close to Deepwater, New Jersey, the Salem River approaches to within two miles of the Delaware River, a distance breached by the Deepwater Canal that connects the two rivers.

From there, the river turns south running along the boundary of Pennsville and Mannington Townships, where it widens into a winding shallow estuary and passes the city of Salem, its head of navigability. The Salem River flows into the Delaware River from the east near the head of Delaware Bay about two miles west of Salem and about five miles southeast of Finns Point, New Jersey.

Like the Salem River, Alloway Creek, a 23.2-mile-long tributary of the Delaware River, is located in Salem County, southwestern New Jersey. The headwaters of the creek are to the southeast of Daretown, in Upper Pittsgrove Township. Entering a marshy area, it meets an unnamed tributary and flows under Alloway Road. Here the creek enters Alloway Lake, created by a dam at the town of Alloway and the biggest lake in Salem County.

Underneath the dam at Alloway, the creek becomes a tidal marsh and meadow estuary. The meanders of the creek become pronounced as the creek turns to run southwest towards Quinton, where it receives the outlet of Laurel Lake, the water supply for Salem. The Alloway Creek Watershed is 75 square miles, encompassing about 20% of Salem County Land Area, and providing an essential habitat for commercial and recreational fishing, trapping and hunting.

Assunpink Creek is another tributary of the Delaware River in western New Jersey. Flowing westward, it enters the Assunpink Wildlife Management Area, where it has been dammed to create Rising Sun Lake. After an unnamed tributary enters from the south, it enters another reservoir, Assunpink Lake.

Beneath Assunpink Lake, the creek runs under Old York Road and moves into Mercer County. The creek now turns northwest, passing under the New Jersey Turnpike and then U.S. Route 130, just southwest of Windsor. Further northwest, the creek flows under Quaker Bridge Road and Interstate 295 before turning southwest and paralleling the Delaware and Raritan Canal. Then the creek runs past the Trenton Train Station and finally empties into the Delaware River in Trenton.

Next there's Cooper River, another Delaware River tributary located in southwestern New Jersey. The confluence of the Cooper River with the Delaware River is in Camden. This river serves as a border between Cherry Hill and Haddon Township, Haddonfield Borough, and Lawnside Borough.

The Cooper River, also known upstream near Haddonfield as Cooper's Creek, was named after the Cooper family, who were some of the original European settlers in the area of Camden County, New Jersey. This Delaware River tributary is 16 miles long measuring from its headwater in Gibbsboro and its watershed is forty square miles.

Fishing in the Cooper River has recently improved since the installation of fish ladders along the impoundment. During season, smallmouth bass and sunfish can be caught in this tributary of the Delaware River.

Besides Cooper River, one will discover another tributary of the Delaware called Crosswicks Creek. Crosswicks Creek is located in Burlington County in western New Jersey. The Crosswicks Creek Watershed encompasses parts of Burlington, Mercer, Monmouth and Ocean counties. The creek's headwaters flow from the Fort Dix and McGuire Air Force Base Military Reserves in a northwesterly direction and then turn sharply south where it joins the Delaware River at the City of Bordentown. With jets flying overhead and shells being test fired, the Crosswicks Creek Watershed has a set of special concerns and is the focus of many protection and restoration activities.

Today, the New Jersey Department of Transportation opened the I-295 extension which has had a huge impact on the Hamilton Marsh, located close to the mouth of the Crosswicks. However, despite development, the vastness of the marsh and peacefulness of Crosswicks Creek still remained. In fact, many canoeists in the area recently claimed they saw wildlife that included herons, egrets, kingfishers, and feathered denizens along the creek.

Yet another tributary is Paulins Kill, also known as Paulinskill River, which is a 28.6-mile-long tributary of the Delaware River located in northwestern New Jersey. Paulins Kill is New Jersey's third largest contributor (behind the Musconetcong River and Maurice River) to the Delaware River in terms of long-term median flow (flowing at a rate of 76 cubic feet of water per second. Paulins Kill also drains an area of 176.85 square miles across parts of New Jersey's Sussex and Warren counties. The Paulins Kill, which moves southwest from its source near Newton, NJ, is located at the border of the Appalachians and New York-New Jersey Highlands physiographic provinces.

In addition to the Delaware's tributaries in New York, Pennsylvania, New Jersey, and Delaware, there are three significant reservoirs that represent part of the Delaware River in the state of New York. These reservoirs are named Neversink Reservoir, Cannonsville Reservoir, and Pepacton Reservoir.

Neversink Reservoir is one of many reservoirs in the Catskill Mountains that supply water to New York City (NYC) and other communities along its water supply network. Neversink Reservoir is located in New York State and lies in Sullivan County's Town of Neversink, which is 75 miles northwest of New York City.

The Neversink River, the longest tributary of the Delaware River, feeds the reservoir. In turn, water collected in the reservoir goes through the Neversink Tunnel, which is a short distance east to Rondout Reservoir that provides almost half of New York City's daily water consumption.

Regarding the reservoir's history, construction started in 1941, as New York City realized that after World War II, it would need to increase its water supply to meet its population growth. Neversink was chosen despite opposition from the area's trout fishermen. Neversink Reservoir was completed in 1953 and started sending water the following year. In 1955, it reached its planned capacity.

Another primary reservoir of the Delaware River is Cannonsville Reservoir. Cannonsville is a reservoir in Delaware County, New York that was created by impounding over half of the West Branch of the Delaware River. It is the westernmost of

New York City's reservoirs, being at the western section of the Delaware Watershed. The reservoir was originally placed in service in 1964, making it the most recently built New York City-owned reservoir. The town of Cannonsville, New York was destroyed to make room for Cannonsville Reservoir. The reservoir sits within the New York towns of Tompkins and Deposit.

It has the biggest drainage basin of all the NYC reservoirs, being at 455 square miles. The reservoir's capacity is 95.7 billion gallons. This water then flows over halfway through the reservoir to enter the 44-mile West Delaware Tunnel in Tompkins, New York. Then it flows through the aqueduct into the Roundout Reservoir, where the water goes into the 85-mile Delaware Aqueduct.

The third New York State-based reservoir of the Delaware River is called the Pepacton Reservoir. Pepacton Reservoir, also known as the Downsville Reservoir or the Downsville Dam, is a reservoir in Delaware County, New York. Impounding over 1/4 of the East Branch of the Delaware River first created this reservoir. In 1942, New York City purchased the valley by the reservoir displacing 974 people, destroying four towns (Arena, Pepacton, Shavertown and Union Grove), and submerging almost half of the Delaware and Northern Railroad in the process. In 1954, the dam at Downsville, New York was completed and the flooding was finished in 1955.

The reservoir is 12 miles south of the village of Delhi, New York and is 101 miles northwest of New York City. It contains about 140.2 billion gallons of water at full capacity and is over 160 feet deep at maximum. These impressive statistics make Pepacton Reservoir New York City's largest reservoir by volume. Pepacton Reservoir supplies New York City with almost 25% of its drinking water. The water moves through the aqueduct into the Rondout Reservoir and empties into the 85-mile Delaware Aqueduct. The water then goes into the Kensico Reservoir in New York's Westchester and Putnam counties just north of The Bronx. Pepacton Reservoir positively impacts the local economy of Downsville, New York, as thousands of tourists travel to Downsville every year to fish for trout.

CHAPTER 1
Wetlands, Aquatic Plants, Fish, Other Wildlife and Its Overall Ecosystem

Originating from its headwaters in the Catskill Mountains of New York and Pocono Mountains of Pennsylvania, to its mouth at the coast, the Delaware River Basin encompasses more than one million acres of wetlands. These wetlands support vital services to society and are an important part of the Delaware Watershed. Healthy wetlands serve as filters, improving downriver and/or downstream water quality. In addition, they decrease flooding and provide crucial habitat for wildlife. Wetlands of the Delaware Watershed make it one of the most dramatic bird regions on the East Coast.

The Delaware River flows to about 330 miles and drains sections of southeast New York state, almost all of eastern Pennsylvania, western New Jersey, and most of eastern Delaware. Along its banks there is a rich array of wetland types, ranging from tidal salt marshes close to the mouth to wooded headwater wetlands in the river's upper stretches. In between there are cattail marshes, shrub thickets, southern hardwood swamps, white cedar bogs, floodplain forests, and seep springs.

There are many different kinds of wetlands but all are classified by having soil that is inundated, saturated, or submerged during part or all of the year and where vegetation is adjusted to growing under wet conditions. A fabulous display of plants and animals inhabit the wetlands of the Delaware Watershed, including a huge number of endangered and rare species that include bald eagles, bog turtles, and rose pogonia orchids. In New Jersey alone, wetlands host over 34 pairs of nesting bald eagles.

At the mouth of Delaware Bay, you can watch spectacular bird migrations along the New Jersey and Delaware coastlines. Each spring, little shorebirds, no larger than a sparrow, make a pit stop along Delaware Bay beaches on their journey north to Arctic breeding grounds. Wildlife officials and scientists estimate that every year up to 1 million shorebirds, which include red knot, ruddy turnstone, sanderling, and dunlin participate in this lengthy migration. Delaware Bay supports a critical rest stop for the birds and an opportunity for them to feed themselves to complete the next leg of their trip.

The shorebirds' stopover along the Delaware Bay happens at the same time that horseshoe crabs in the region lay their eggs. The Delaware Estuary is the biggest staging area for shorebirds in the Atlantic Flyway and is the second largest staging site in North America. From mid-May until early June, migratory shorebirds land in Delaware Bay during the peak of horse crab mating season. At least eleven species of migratory birds use horseshoe crab eggs to replenish their food supply during their trip from South American wintering areas to Arctic breeding grounds.

Horseshoe crab eggs are also a seasonal food item of finfish. In the Delaware River from May to August, striped bass and white perch eat horseshoe crab eggs. In addition, American eel, silver perch, kingfish, and flounder eat the crab's eggs and larvae.

In the Delaware River Region, Atlantic loggerhead turtles eat adult horseshoe crabs. Scientists found that horseshoe crabs represented up to 42 percent of the loggerhead turtles' diet from the Chesapeake Bay off the Atlantic Ocean.

Yet despite how shorebirds and horseshoe crabs benefit the ecology of the Delaware River Region, scientific researchers indicated that the number of adult horseshoe crabs in the area has decreased 75 percent in the past eleven years. Thus the number of crab eggs available to foraging shorebirds has declined significantly. So based upon the declines in shorebirds and horseshoe crabs, researchers predict that the Red knot (New Jersey State threatened shorebird) population migrating to the mouth of the Delaware River (Delaware Bay Area) will eventually become extinct.

One specific wetland area that is important to life along the Delaware River Area is the Hamilton/Trenton Marshes Region in New Jersey. Half of this 1,250-acre site is tidal and encompasses an ancient winding course of the Delaware River where one can see man-made, riverine, and natural wetlands.

Tidal influence on the Delaware River occurs as far north as Trenton, New Jersey where tidal amplitude is over six feet. Most of the eastern bank of the Delaware River is a cobble shore and water movement is typically too fast for the growth of many big plants. However, plant species such as New York Ironwood and Sneezeweed may be found there. Plants such as wild rice and subulate arrowhead also grow in the Hamilton/Trenton Marsh Area. Generally, marshes in that region support habitat for birds such as least bitterns, marsh wrens, yellowthroats, and red-winged blackbirds.

Additional sources of wetlands in the Hamilton/Trenton Marshes are ponded areas Ponds near the Delaware River provide homes to aquatic plants, frogs, turtles, and wading birds. The aquatic plant life includes creeping water primrose, mermaid-weed, and water lily. Frogs such as pickerel frogs, New Jersey chorus frogs, green frogs and bullfrogs also live in that wetland region. Turtles there consist of snapping turtle and others include bog turtles, red-eared, eastern painted and red-bellied turtles. Wading birds found there are green herons, great-blue herons, wood ducks, ring-necked ducks and geese. Other birds in that area include red-tailed hawk, upland sandpiper, northern harrier, and redheaded woodpecker. Moreover, bald eagle and osprey can be seen nesting on top of riverside perches while peregrine falcons inhabit the highest, steepest banks overseeing the river.

Wetlands in the Hamilton/Trenton Marshes also consist of wet forests. Trees in these forests include sweet gum, red maple, box elder, white ash, and willows. Walk along these trees and you will typically see plants like fern, Virginia creeper, poison ivy, cabbage, and grapevines. Plantlife in this region also consist of wildflowers. Some of these flowers include sweet peas, daisies, day lilies, wild columbine, foxglove, Joe-Pye weed, jewelweed and primroses. Animals found in these wet woods are white-tailed deer, raccoons, chipmunk, and gray squirrels.

In the Upper Delaware, many insects reside there, which represent the area's food chain. Specifically, three types of well-known aquatic insects that inhabit the upper river include Mayflies, Caddis flies, and Stoneflies. As a whole, many of the Delaware River's water-dwelling insects such as these flies are a critical part of the river's ecosystem.

Regarding Mayflies, there are more than 700 species of these insects that live in the Delaware River and throughout North America. Mayflies spend almost their entire life inhabiting water, such as in the Delaware, in the larval stage. The majority of Mayfly nymphs require clean, well-oxygenated environments, but some species live in lakes. Upon reaching maturity the adults' life span as a terrestrial is short, ranging from an hour to three days depending upon the species. Unlike Caddis flies and Stoneflies, once Mayflies emerge from the nymph stage, they lack mouthparts and don't eat after leaving the water. Although most Mayfly species have a seasonal, univoltine life cycle, some do have multiple broods during the same season.

Caddis flies are the biggest group of aquatic insects found in the Delaware River. In fact, about 12,000 species inhabit North America. By far, Caddis is also the most complex insect, with each genus widely varying in type of case and pupation habits. Some construct portable cases, and abandon them, building new ones as they grow while other flies build fixed cases. Whereas some Caddis flies are free living and don't construct cases until their final instar. Cases are made from different materials and are affixed to the substrate by the use of spinning silk thread. The majority of Caddis hatches are thickest during warm sunny days. The sunlight triggers the hatch by forming a greenhouse like effect through the water thus warming the larval case.

Most Caddis species have a univoltine life cycle and only a few have multiple young during the same season. Adults live for a few days to about two months after mating and egg laying flights. Grown-up Caddis flies find sustenance by feeding on plant matter and pollen. They also inhabit a diverse range of environments, as some species are much more tolerant of river or other water pollution than are Mayflies and Stoneflies.

Stoneflies are also plentiful in the Upper Delaware and about 500 species of these insects live in North America. Immature insects of most species live in riffles because they need much oxygenated water to survive. However, other species inhabit slower, silt-bottomed, warm water streams or rivers (like the Delaware) while others live in ponds and lakes.

Most Stoneflies are mainly carnivores in the larval stage, especially the later stages of some bigger species. Others eat on debris consuming the bacteria and fungus developed by deteriorating leaves. Moreover, almost all kinds of Stoneflies have a univoltine life cycle while some have multiple broods during the same season. Life spans of adults differ between species from three days up to a few weeks. Adult flies with a short life span don't feed once they emerge from the nymph stage. Other types of adult

Stoneflies with longer life spans get nourishment from plants, pollen, and other growth found on the bark of trees.

Besides aquatic insects and other life forms found in American rivers such as the Potomac, Hudson, and Charles rivers, the Delaware River also supports a very large number of fish species.

Some of the Delaware's popular native fish species, which often congregate and migrate into the river, include river herring (blueback and alewife), shad (hickory, American and gizzard), American eel, bay anchovy, shortnose sturgeon, striped bass, weakfish, catfish (channel and white), redfin pickerel, chain pickerel, muskellunge, sunfish, and trout (brook, rainbow, and brown).

In New York State, the Hudson River is home to all members of the herring family. Freshwater sections of New York's Delaware River also receive herring runs, but only after the fish have migrated through bordering states.

Blueback herring, also known as river herring, live most of their life in the ocean. However, they migrate to freshwater rivers and streams to spawn. In the Delaware Estuary, you can find plenty of blueback herring in the upper area of the estuary. In addition, a huge number of bluebacks go to the Lower Delaware River to spawn.

Adult blueback herring reproduce from spring to early summer in upstream freshwater or brackish regions of rivers and tributaries (includes the Delaware River and its tributaries). Spawning occurs in the evening in rapid, strong currents over a hard substance. After spawning, adults swim downstream and return to the ocean. Eggs float close to the rocky bottom of the river for two to four days until hatching, depending on temperature. At hatching, blueback herring larvae are .12 to .20 inches. Larvae become juveniles at about .79 inches or at 25 to 35 days. When young bluebacks turn about one month old, they head for salt water. Bluebacks feed on zooplankton, fish eggs, shrimp and small fish.

Another river herring is the alewife. Like blueback herring, alewife lives mostly in the ocean and migrates into freshwater rivers and streams to spawn. In April and May, these fish enter to spawn in rivers (like the Delaware River) in areas of rivers where slow currents and shallow water are located. Like blueback herring, alewife can stand different substrates such as sand, mud, gravel, and boulders. Eggs and sperm belonging to both the alewife and blueback herring are released in the water column where fertilization takes place. Eggs remain suspended in the water column until eggs hatch. After spawning, grown-up alewives live in the shallow Delaware Estuary until autumn, before returning to the ocean for the winter.

In addition to herring, there's shad. Shad is a kind of fish that once was common in the Philadelphia, Pennsylvania area. The region of Philadelphia relied on this fish for their economic sustenance in the colonial times and up until World War I. One year over 4 million shad were caught from the Delaware River, but shad has not always been that plentiful. Like many fish today, shad is over fished. In fact during 1806, overfishing of shad was so bad the state of Pennsylvania had to ban the use of gill nets.

In New York State, shad come from stocks in the Delaware and Hudson rivers and are part of the mid-Atlantic population. In regards to anglers in New York State, fishing for shad on the Delaware River is different than on the Hudson River. Because the Upper Delaware is much clearer and smaller than the Hudson, shad are more visible to fishermen. Shad can be taken by fly-fishing and best fishing typically happens in the lower East Branch and the main stem from Port Jervis to Hancock, New York.

Anglers also need to know that shad tend to follow the Delaware River's channel because the channel offers the fish the deeper water they appear to prefer and because of its swifter water, a direction to follow.

Moreover, obstructions in the Delaware such as wing dams, bridge trestles, islands, or huge rocks are places where shad will hold for short periods of time to rest. Fishing behind these obstructions is usually productive. The best hours of the day for fishing shad, regardless of weather conditions, are the late afternoon and early evening hours. Shad become more active at this time of the day and may often be seen zigzagging through a pool's tail waters as nighttime approaches. More advice for an angler is once that person has hooked a shad, he or she must not move. There are other fish in the area and even if fishing slacks of for an hour or more, an angler needs to stay at his or her location because that fisherman has found a "shad path" which other schools will soon be following.

There are different kinds of shad and one type that spawns in the Delaware River is hickory shad. This shad is a fish that spends most of its adult life in the ocean. In the spring, hickory shad head to freshwater rivers like the Delaware to reproduce. After reproducing, hickory shad go back to the sea. River currents transport the fertilized eggs, which are then developed into larvae that start to feed 4 to 7 days after hatching. Next larvae wash downstream into tidal freshwater stretches of the spawning rivers, like the Upper Delaware Estuary, and eventually mature into young adults. In the early summer, young shad migrate out of their nursery habitats to the ocean. With water temperatures rising in the spring, adult hickory shad will migrate back to their native rivers (such as the Delaware River) to finish their life cycle.

In addition to hickory shad moving into the Delaware, there are American shad. The American shad is the biggest member of the herring species residing in or visiting Pennsylvania waters like the Delaware River. Adult shad head as far north to the East Branch and West Branch of the Delaware River, in northeastern Pennsylvania.

Female American shad, carrying their eggs during the spawning trip, average 4 to 5 pounds yet it's common to see one weighing 6 or 7 pounds. Males are smaller for their age. Shad can grow to thirty inches, with a maximum weight of about twelve pounds. American shad are colored silver on the sides, with a bluish or greenish-metallic sheen on the back.

Like other anadromous fish, American shad live in the sea as adults. As marine grown-ups, shad swim in schools and travel way upstream to large, freshwater rivers like the Delaware to reproduce. In the spring, shad run upriver from salt water into fresh water during their spawning migration when the river water temperature is in the mid-50s to 60-degree range, with peak spawning occurring at about 65 degrees Fahrenheit.

The males run upriver in schools ahead of the females. Shad spawn in the evening over rocks and sandbars. Females, which are bigger than the males, bear 100,000 eggs on average. American shad eggs are a little bit heavier than water, so they don't readily sink. Instead, they drift along with the current. Depending upon water temperature, the eggs mature and hatch in eight to twelve days. Hatched shad live many months in the fresh water, such as in the Delaware River, reaching the sea by their first autumn. American shad remain in salt water for 4 or 5 years and until they are about eighteen inches long (when they become sexually mature). Shad feed on zooplankton, worms, and tiny fish. While in fresh river water, the young ones feed on insect larvae.

American shad have long been a critical food resource for people living along the Delaware River. Over four hundred years ago, the Lenape (or Delaware) tribe depended on the migration of the shad as a staple of their diet. They harvested the fish and prepared them in many ways. Some fish were grilled quickly on wooden racks and others were prepared for later use by air drying or smoking them. Early European settlers also depended on shad for their diets.

Last but not least is the gizzard shad. The gizzard shad differs from the hickory and American shad by its gizzard like stomach that helps process the plant food and plankton this fish squeezes from the water. Its back is silvery blue-green to gray and its sides are silvery or reflect green, blue, or reddish tints. Although this shad is a school fish and has a common herring species body shape, it also has a short dorsal fin located on the middle of its back.

Gizzard shad live and migrate to fresh and brackish waters throughout America that include the Delaware River and its tributaries. During the spring and early summer is when these fish reproduce; however, they don't have a consistent spawning migration pattern, except that these fish in brackish or salt water return to fresh water. Gizzard shad spawn mostly in low gradient ditches or tributaries, where huge spawning groups move upstream as far as water depth will allow, to spawn in shallow water normally less than five feet deep. The shad's spawning period ranges from two weeks to two months. Habitat conditions are best for gizzard shad in warm, shallow bodies of water with soft, mud bottoms and high turbidity with few predators. Gizzard shad mainly feed on plankton.

Besides shad, American eel are part of the ecosystem supporting life within the Delaware River Estuary. In fact, the Delaware River has the biggest eel population of all streams and rivers in Pennsylvania. American eel spend most of their lives in the Delaware Estuary, other estuaries and in freshwater streams. These eel are capable of migrating upstream and/or upriver despite many barriers such as low dams, falls, and spillways that are impassable to other migratory fish.

In the Mid-Atlantic Region, American eel remain eight to twenty-four years in estuaries or freshwater streams before they return to their birthplace in the Sargasso Sea to spawn. The eel reproduce in winter and early spring. American eel can live in many different habitats and have a very big geographic range. During the evening, they migrate and scour for food. Adult eel feed on mollusks, insects, worms, crustaceans, and other fish.

Another popular fish in both the Delaware Bay and Estuary is the bay anchovy. Bay anchovy are little, schooling fish, which are plentiful in the Delaware Bay. They have great ecological importance in the Mid-Atlantic Region, as they are eaten by many recreation and commercial fish, as well as birds. In the Delaware Estuary, the bay anchovy's spawning season is from the beginning of April until the middle of June. Their eggs are found at different depths but are mostly concentrated near the surface. The majority of the young migrates out of the estuaries at the end of the summer in schools, and can be discovered in huge numbers on the inner continental shelf in the autumn. The average size for adults is about three inches and bay anchovy only live for one or two years. In the Delaware Bay, these fish mainly eat copepods and the adults endure a wide range of water temperatures and salinities.

In addition to bay anchovy, there is the shortnose sturgeon. The shortnose sturgeon spends most of its life in brackish or salt water and heads upstream in coastal rivers, which include the Delaware River, to reproduce. Migration happens in winter and spring, so that they arrive at the spawning grounds when the water temperature is between 8 and 9 degrees Celsius. During May and June, adults relocate downstream or downriver. These particular sturgeons take a long time to mature. For example, the age of the first spawning in the Delaware River is between seven and ten years.

Both the young and grown-ups are bottom feeders and eat an array of bivalves, crustaceans, and worms. Shortnose sturgeons are also slow growing fish. Yet once they become adults, they reach body lengths of about forty inches. Even though these sturgeons mature late in life, they can live anywhere from 15 to 20 years and are highly fertile, with their total egg production rising proportionally to body size.

Young shortnose sturgeons stay in freshwater for their initial summer of life and then move to deeper, more brackish water in winter. A large part of the Delaware River's shortnose sturgeon population overwinter between Roebling, New Jersey and Trenton, New Jersey from December to March. Then in mid to late March, most adults move upriver to spawn.

Spawning happens between late March and early May from the river's New Jersey portions of Trenton Rapids to Scudders Falls. The sturgeons' eggs are found on or close to the bottom of the Delaware and are adhesive. The eggs hatch about 13 days after fertilization. Once the fish have spawned, they swim downriver close to Philadelphia, Pennsylvania, where they will remain throughout the month of May. After May, the shortnose sturgeon fish will relocate back upriver to the overwintering ground (also called a summering area) and stay there through summer and winter.

Sturgeons (both shortnose and Atlantic) were once plentiful in the Delaware River, occurring in massive numbers that greatly exceeded those discovered in the Hudson River. Yet despite those facts, the shortnose sturgeon has been listed as endangered since the beginning of the federal government's Endangered Species Act in 1973.

Although there are presently about 12,000 adult shortnose sturgeon living in the Delaware River Estuary, the fish face serious threats caused by humans. One such threat includes water quality contaminants that have been linked to developmental and reproductive disorders in many fish species. Other human-inflicted threats to Delaware River shortnose sturgeon consist of waterfront development, industrialization, boat/ship strikes, death caused from recreational and commercial fishing, and in river construction projects within the spawning area.

Yet the good news is that recent work confirmed from researchers and biologists confirmed successful reproduction of shortnose sturgeon covering an 11-mile stretch of the lower non-tidal Delaware River. Meanwhile, environmentalists identified crucial spawning/nursery grounds by capturing early life stages (eggs and larvae) utilizing artificial plankton nets and substrates over two seasons.

Moreover, researchers will track young and adult sturgeon with tags to determine movement patterns and habitat use in the

Delaware River. This new research will be added to existing data on the migration of shortnose sturgeon. The research will also help biologists develop protection strategies and eventually prevent more declines of this fish species.

In addition to shortnose sturgeons, biologists in Delaware reported some bad news about the Atlantic sturgeon fish species. In 2010, they reported that there were no signs of baby sturgeons in the Delaware River.

Today, climate change, pollution, and cargo ships that navigate up the James River in Virginia, Delaware River in the Pennsylvania/New Jersey Region, and Hudson River in New York are big threats to shortnose sturgeons and Atlantic sturgeons.

As for the fish's appearance, sturgeons don't look like most fish. They don't have scales but have armor-like scutes (like scales but produce a horny outer layer) and date back 120 million years. In the Delaware River, the precise spawning area for sturgeon is evasive, perhaps somewhere north of Wilmington, Delaware.

During the fall of 2010, the National Oceanographic and Atmospheric Administration announced the proposal to list sturgeon as endangered in the Delaware/Hudson Range, the Chesapeake and other locations. The listing is geared towards saving the fish's habitat, as their harvest already is banned.

The Delaware River is also home to rock bass and striped bass. The rock bass, a member of the sunfish family, has a short, robust body with green top and gold or brassy-colored sides. Its scales have a dark spot, often creating a striped-like appearance.

Rock bass are native to the Delaware and Connecticut rivers. Rock bass are typically found near sheltered pool areas around woody debris and rocks close to the mountains and foothills along the Delaware River. These bass eat mainly insects, small fish, and crayfish.

In addition to rock bass, plenty of striped bass live in the Delaware. In fact, along the Atlantic coastline, the main spawning areas for striped bass are in the Delaware and Hudson rivers. Striped bass spawning normally occurs over sandy to muddy substances in currents turbulent enough to keep fertilized eggs suspended in the water stack until hatching occurs. Migration to the spawning grounds is caused when water temperatures rise to about 18 degrees Celsius. From April through June, spawning typically happens in water temperatures of about 11 degrees to 26 degrees Celsius.

When the eggs are hatched, larvae scour on zooplankton and are transported downriver to higher salinities where they will remain in the river system for up to three years. Young striped bass utilize habitats for rearing such as estuaries and inshore areas with rocky shorelines, deep trenches, or sandy beaches. In the Delaware River, juvenile-of-year migrate downriver from their spawning grounds to tidal sections of the rivers to spend their first summer. Striped bass, also called "stripers," can spend two or more years within the Delaware Estuary before they meet the offshore migratory population. In addition, despite past pollution problems that almost eliminated striped bass from the Delaware, their population recovered after the river's water quality was improved. From 1998 to 2003, the striped bass harvest has remained at about 2,500,000 to 3,500,000 fish.

Case in point, the Delaware River is the longest, undammed river east of the Mississippi. That means striped bass and shad (two of its native fish species) can swim easily (without hitting any obstructions) from the Atlantic Ocean and the Delaware River to spawn in a lot of freshwater tributaries and wetlands of the Upper Delaware. This is due to the fact that the majority of fish can't jump over a dam.

Weakfish represent another fish that has made a home in the Delaware Bay and Delaware River. These fish are well known as a recreational fishing target in the Delaware Bay and surrounding shoreline.

In the spring, weakfish reproduce in the Delaware Estuary and typically move north as far as Massachusetts for the summer. During the winter, these same fish migrate as far south as Cape Hatteras, North Carolina and the East Coast of Florida.
Weakfish prefer shallow waters and sandy bottoms. They normally feed throughout the water column on small invertebrates, shrimp, and fish.

Weakfish grow fast and mature between one and two years of age. Estuaries, such as the Delaware, provide feeding spots and spawning areas for adult weakfish, and are equally significant as nursery regions for the young ones. Weakfish mainly feed on crustaceans, shrimp, and tiny fish that are found close to eelgrass beds.

Yet another fish found in the Delaware River are channel catfish. Channel catfish are plentiful in the river. Both the Upper and Lower Delaware River has large catfish populations.

Channel cats have smooth scales that are speckled, with a darker back to a light whitish belly. Their colors can differ from black, to blue, or olive. Generally, in muddy water they are olive to yellowish white and in clear water they are blacker in color. Males typically have larger heads than females and males have darker-colored bodies than females. Channels are often found at the bottom of the Delaware and they prefer muddy surface bottoms and clear water.

Channel catfish spawn in the summer. After hatching the baby cats take from two days to two weeks until they become independent. Channel cats make nests in hidden places such as under overhangs, in enclosed cans or in deep holes that give them extra protection from predators.

The parents of channel catfish invest a lot into their offspring. After spawning the male chases the female away from the nest but she does not leave completely and will protect her eggs from a distance. The male and female will also attack predators and chase them away with an open mouth but will not eat them. The male provides the young with a source of food by burrowing. Burrowing is a process where the fish swim down into the mud on the bottom of the water and thrash from side to side stirring up food particles for the offspring to eat. The female supplies food for the young cats by positioning her body about a meter above the nest and then releasing eggs for her babies to eat.

In addition to channel catfish, white catfish are native species of the Delaware River. White cats are members of the bullhead group of catfishes. The fish are normally blue-gray in color above, fading to gray on their sides with a white belly, hence the name. White catfish are sometimes mistaken for channel catfish, but white cats have much wider heads and lack black spots on its sides. Although white cats are common in the Delaware River, they are often overlooked. This may be in part to their small size compared to channel, flathead, and blue catfish. However, these fish are aggressive feeders and have a tendency to feed more during the daytime than other catfish.

Catching a variety of catfish in the Delaware can be tricky for anglers depending upon the time of year they fish. Fishermen need to be aware that during winter when the weather is cold, they need to fish in shallower water closer to the shore. That is where they will find the catfish as they are relocating to find their sources of food. Anglers will also find that catfish feed less often in the colder weather. However, during the summer as the weather gets warmer, the catfish's prey fish will swim into deeper areas and the cats will have to follow them there. Fishermen will also see that in warm weather they are better off fishing for catfish at night than during the daylight hours.

Moving on from catfish, there is the redfin pickerel. In Pennsylvania, redfin are small pickerel that are commonly found in the Delaware River Watershed. The redfin is one of the smallest members of the pike species, growing only up to twelve inches. This pickerel is greenish gray to dark olive-bronze on the back, with shading down its sides. The stomach is tinted white or yellow and its snout is broad and short. Its fins are unspotted and reddish, providing its common name.

In springtime, redfins spawn when the water temperature reads approximately 50 degrees Fahrenheit. Their eggs are discovered randomly in the shallows above submerged aquatic vegetation and other organic debris. Redfin's eggs hatch in about two weeks and receive no parental care. Unlike bigger pikes, the redfin does not include fish as a main part of its diet. Instead, it feeds on crayfish, aquatic insects, and small crustaceans.

In addition to redfin pickerel, chain pickerel are abundant in Pennsylvania waters. In Pennsylvania, chain pickerel are limited to the Delaware, Susquehanna and Potomac watersheds. They are most commonly found in the glaciated Pocono northeast.

Chain pickerel can grow to over thirty inches long and weigh up to five pounds. However, 2-pound pickerel are most common. Chain pickerel hide easily in its weedy habitat, with its dark, greenish-yellow back, fading to lighter yellow-green along its sides. These pike have a long snout and as is common of pickerel, both the cheek and gill cover are fully scaled.

These kinds of pickerel are commonly found in the sluggish parts of clear streams and in the acidic waters that drain boggy wetlands, as in northeastern Pennsylvania. Chain pickerel like to live in shallow water and they can tolerate a wide water temperature range.

Early spring is when chain pickerel spawn as water temperatures are typically in the upper 40s to low 50s F. The reproduction period lasts about one week. Their sticky eggs, 6,000 t o 8,000 normally deposited by each female, are scattered above underwater weeds.

Newly hatched chain pickerel attach themselves to plant stems during the absorption of the yolk sac. The young munch on aquatic insects and are eaten by bigger fish. As they get older, chain pickerel consume more fish that become their main diet. Adults are solitary predators that swim through under river weedbeds to catch their prey that include other fish, huge aquatic insects, crayfish, frogs, and other little animal life that gets into the water. At a year old, chain pickerel are about seven inches long and after four years, they grow to approximately fifteen inches. Their natural lifespan is eight to ten years.

In addition to pickerel, muskellunge, also known as "muskie" or "musky," live in northern waters such as the Delaware. Muskies represent the biggest members of the pike family and look like the northern pike and American pickerel in appearance and behavior. Just like other pikes, a musky has an elongate body, flat head and dorsal with pelvic and anal fins set way back on its body. Muskellunge can reach lengths of 2 to 4.9 feet and weights of more than 66 pounds although some have grown to 7 feet long and weighed 100 pounds. The fish are a light silver, green or brown with dark vertical stripes on the flank that may tend to break up into spots. In some instances, markings may be absent, especially in fish from turbid waters.

Muskellunge prefer living in water where they lurk along weed edges, rocky outcrops or other structures to rest. During the summer, a musky creates two distinct home ranges (a shallow range and a deeper one). The shallow range is typically much smaller than the deeper one due to shallow water heating up. A muskie continuously patrols the ranges in search of food within the appropriate conditions of water temperature. An adult musky is an ambush predator with large, needle-like, razor-sharp teeth that preys upon just about anything that fits into its mouth. Although most of its diet consists of fish it also includes crayfish, frogs, ducklings, snakes, muskrats, mice, other small mammals, and even small birds.

Regarding its lifestyle and behavior, muskies sometimes form small schools in certain territories and the fish spawn in mid to late spring over shallow, vegetated areas. Muskellunge prefer a sand or rock bottom for spawning so that the eggs do not sink into the mud and suffocate. Males arrive first and attempt to establish dominance over a territory. Spawning can last from five to ten days and that usually happens in the evenings. The surviving embryos not eaten by insects, other fish or crayfish normally hatch within two weeks.

Besides muskellunge and other pike, the Delaware River is home to sunfish; these fish are also called "sunnies." Sunfish are widespread and plentiful in the Delaware where the river's most commonly fished species are Bluegill, Pumpkinseed, and the Redbreast.

These three sunfish species are all brightly colored, especially during the months of June to August when they are spawning. The male sunfish clears gravel nests in the river so the female can deposit her eggs in it. Sunfish spawn when water temperatures reach 68 degrees Fahrenheit, normally in 1 to 3 feet of water. Color and differences in their gill flaps differentiate these fish. The bluegill has a black, rounded gill flap, the pumpkinseed has a black gill flap with a bright red-orange tip, and the redbreast has a long gill flap with a black spot at its tip.

Many northern rivers (like the Delaware) and streams that warm during the summer have very good fishable populations of the three mentioned sunfish species. In fact, their eagerness to bite and energy make sunfish great entertainment for a family-fishing trip on a nice "sunny" day.

The redbreast is typically found with smallmouth bass and rock bass in habitats like reservoirs, small creeks, and rivers. Redbreasts are also more active in cooler waters than pumpkinseeds and bluegills. The season for anglers to fish for sunfish is year round in the Delaware River and other waters. However, May to October is when water temperatures are between 60 and 80 degrees F, which appear to be the best months of the year to catch them. Moreover, the most well-known way to catch sunfish is with a hook and bobber. A fisherman doesn't need high technical gear for these fish.

Finally, last but not least on my fish list are trout. In the Delaware River, all trout are classified as wild fish, spawned in the tributaries. In Pennsylvania, brook trout, also called "brookies," is Pennsylvania's official state fish. Brook trout are the only stream trout that are native to Pennsylvania.

The body color of the brook trout is normally dark green. Its back is dark olive-green or gray-green. The sides and belly are lighter, sometimes with gray, green or even lavender tones with additional irregular marks. The fins are pale to bright orange with a white leading edge followed by a black stripe. Moreover, the tail of the brook trout is less forked than that of most trout and salmon.

Brook trout generally inhabit Pennsylvania and are commonly found in watersheds that include the Delaware, Ohio, Susquehanna, Genesee, and Potomac rivers. These trout are also found throughout Pennsylvania as hatchery-raised, stocked fish. Brook trout can live in acidic waters as long as temperatures don't exceed much over 65 degrees Fahrenheit.

From mid-September to November, brook trout reproduce and may migrate to upstream headwaters to find the ideal spawning spot. Like other trout, with violent motion of the body and tail, the female digs a shallow nest in the bottom gravel where there is good water flow to bring oxygen to the eggs. After fertilization, the eggs receive a little more covering of gravel and then are given no more parental care. Eggs develop during the winter and hatch in late winter or early spring. A brook trout more than eighteen inches long may produce about 4,000 eggs. Huge brook trout caught by fishermen in Pennsylvania are mainly hatchery-stocked fish. These trout feed on insects both beneath and on the water's surface, crustaceans, and small fish. Brook trout are typically short-lived and few of them survive in the wild more than five years.

Brook trout are not the only trout commonly found in the Delaware River. Rainbow trout and brown trout also live there. Rainbow trout are plentiful in the Upper Delaware River and were introduced in the Delaware during the late 1800s. Rainbows are found in isolated pockets throughout the entire Upper Delaware and have become more abundant as you get close to Hancock, New York. Rainbow trout spawn in the spring and coexist nicely with brown trout that share the river with them. Rainbows are hard fighting fish and can grow from 15 to 16 inches long, with some attaining 22 inches or more. The rainbow trout is a wild resident of the Delaware River and is not supported by any hatchery stocking programs.

Like rainbow trout, brown trout is another wild fish in the Delaware. Brown trout spawn in the fall in the river and average about 15 inches in length. Bigger browns can grow up to 23 inches long. Many fishermen catch browns in the Delaware during the early spring. Although brown trout are stocked in parts of the upper East Branch, Beaverkill, Willowemoc, and the Neversink River in New York, they also inhabit the Delaware River and its branches where most of them are wild-bred fish.

In addition to the Delaware River's native fish species, environmentalists and scientists are concerned about invasive fish and plant species in the Delaware. One kind of invasive fish species in particular is the flathead catfish. This catfish is on top of numerous "least wanted" invasive fish species in the Delaware due to its ferocious eating habits, huge size, and ability to swim long distances in a short time.

Under good conditions, flatheads can grow to over 124 pounds. Their bodies are yellowish brown to dark brown with black or brown mottling on lighter brown sides. The flathead catfish has a broadly flattened head and a tail that is only slightly indented, appearing more square or rounded. The key characteristic that helps people distinguish the flathead catfish from other catfish is that the lower jaw of the flathead projects past the upper jaw. The earliest record of flathead catfish in the Delaware River Watershed was in 1991. Since then, populations have spread in the main stem of the Delaware River close to Roebling, New Jersey.

The flathead catfish is a much desired game fish; however, its release into new watersheds has made problems for other fish. There are many impacts that include threats to biodiversity (flatheads compete with native fish for food and habitat). They also prey heavily on crayfish, crabs, young American eels, American shad, and other small fish.

Flatheads are also the cause of human health risks. These catfish tend to accumulate toxins such as polychlorinated biphenyl concentrations (PCBs). For this reason, Pennsylvania officials advise that people eat no more than one meal a month of these fish caught in the Delaware and its tributaries. Finally, flathead catfish have a negative economic impact on the blue crab industry as well as sturgeon, striped bass, and shad.

In addition to flathead catfish, the northern snakehead is another invasive fish species in the Delaware River. Native to Russia, China, North and South Korea, the northern snakehead has been found in several states over the past ten years. It also has been seen in the tidal section of the Delaware River and Potomac River.

Often known as the "Frankenfish" for its ravenous appetite and sharp teeth, snakeheads can weigh up to 15 pounds and is able to adapt to many different aquatic environments. Northern snakehead populations in the Delaware River Area are also increasing. According to the Pennsylvania Fish and Boat Commission, the first snakeheads in Pennsylvania were found in 2004 in Meadow Lake in Philadelphia, which is connected, to the Delaware River via a series of tidal sloughs and embayments. Since then, a breeding population has been established in the Lower Delaware with snakeheads slowly expanding their range northward and into the tributaries of the Delaware River. Moreover, biologists with the New Jersey Division of Fish and Wildlife confirmed that the first snakehead in New Jersey was collected in 2009 from Delaware River tributary Woodbury Creek in Gloucester County.

Today, biologists in both Pennsylvania and New Jersey are monitoring the snakehead's spread since they are predators. However, at this time no one is certain what type of impact northern snakeheads will have on other fish in the Delaware River. Biologists in New Jersey and Pennsylvania confirmed that they would not expect to detect an impact on other fish in the Delaware River until the snakeheads become more abundant. Yet nevertheless, biologists in the Delaware River Region want anglers to report catches so they can document the spread of northern snakeheads.

Yet other non-native fish found in the Delaware River are perch, which are specifically nuisance fish species in the river. Typically, silvery-white in color, hence the names, depending upon size and habitat specimens have begun to develop a darker side near the dorsal fin and along the top of the fish. White perch have been reported up to 19.5 inches long and weighing up to 4.8 pounds. These fish are prolific species as the female can deposit over 140,000 eggs in a spawning session, lasting just over a week.

However, since white perch are invasive fish, they are known to eat the eggs of many fish species native to the Delaware

River, such as walleye (native to Delaware River) and other perches. At times, fish eggs are 100% of the white perch's diet. White perch also prey on eggs of white bass and even eggs of its own species. They eat fish eggs in the spring and are known to eat minnows.

Some states consider the white perch to be a nuisance species due to its ability to destroy fisheries. They have been associated with the declines in both white bass and walleye populations because they dine heavily on baitfish used by those species and outcompete them for food and space. There are even some states that even recommend not releasing captured white perch back into the water to help control its spread.

Besides fish, another invasive species to the Delaware is Didymo. Didymo, also called "rock snot," is a non-native, invasive microscopic algae (diatom) that can make huge amounts of stalk material to create thick brown mats on river bottoms. Didymo is a threat to the Delaware River's biodiversity and aquatic habitat.

Unlike other aquatic invasive plants, Didymo grows on the bottom of both still and flowing waters. It is known to develop mat-like growths (blooms) that can last for months. During blooms, the mats can completely cover long stretches of riverbeds, changing river conditions and choking out many of the organisms that live on the bottom of the Delaware River. This invasive plant can affect trout and other fish by limiting their food source.

Didymo has been found near the Catskill Mountains in the West Branch Delaware River under Cannonsville Reservoir (Delaware County), East Branch Delaware River beneath Pepacton Reservoir (Delaware County, and the main Delaware River (Delaware and Sullivan Counties).

Another fact regarding Didymo is that presently there are no known ways for controlling or eliminating it once it infests a water body like the Delaware River. To prevent the spread of Didymo, fishermen, kayakers and boaters are urged to use the "Inspect, Clean and Dry" method to limit the spread of this invasive algae.

Besides native or nonnative fish and plants, many blue crabs inhabit the Delaware River. Blue crabs are also plentiful in New York's Hudson River. The color above the blue crab is typically olive or bluish-green. Their claws are bright blue, their last pair of legs is paddle shaped and their shell is twice as wide as it is long. These crabs pass through about twenty molts until they become adults. Blue crabs reach maturity after 18 months and they live to up to three years.

Mating happens immediately after puberty molt and there is a complex courtship. The females mate just once a year and each occurrence produce two to three broods of eggs. Within each brood there are millions of eggs that always hatch in darkness and high tide. Blue crabs eat crustaceans and little fish. They are also tolerant of high temperatures and have been discovered in water exceeding 95 degrees Fahrenheit. Furthermore, the blue crab supports the most significant inshore fishery in the Delaware River, Hudson River, and throughout the Middle Atlantic Region.

Chapter 2
Delaware River's Pollution Issues, Preventive Measures/ Solutions and Flood/Climate Change Concerns

Although the Delaware River is now one of the cleanest rivers in America, American Rivers, a Washington, D.C.-based advocacy group, stated in 2010 that natural gas drilling in the Delaware River Basin has now made the Upper Delaware River the most endangered river in the United States. According to American Rivers, the fast growth of hydro fracturing poses a huge threat to the Upper Delaware and its tributaries. During hydro fracturing, drillers inject a mixture of chemicals, water, and sand at high presser down a well bore and into the surrounding rock, making fractures that release natural gas reserves. The chemicals used in the "fracking" process pose an environmental threat to groundwater.

In addition to gas drilling, now point and non-point source pollution is the main reason for degraded streams within the Delaware Watershed. Point source pollution is pollution dumped from a pipe or some discrete conveyance. Two examples of point source polluters are industrial discharges and sewage treatment plants. Non-point source pollution is pollution that is washed into our waters over a wide area. Examples of nonpoint source pollutants include petroleum products from parking lots and streets, agricultural run-off from fields and pens, and acidic mine outflows.

Besides gas drilling, point and non-point pollution, pollution from urbanization and industry has taken its toll on the river since the 1700s. Early settlers on the Delaware dumped raw sewage into the river, which left thousands of people dead each year from waterborne diseases. The Delaware Estuary is impacted by the lack of water clarity and toxic contaminants associated with urbanization and industrialization. Then as years passed, industrialization increased in the watershed making it a much polluted area.

In 1940, the health of the Delaware River was so poor that the Interstate Commission on the Delaware River Basin called the tidal river below Trenton, New Jersey at Philadelphia, Pennsylvania and Camden, New Jersey "one of the most grossly polluted areas in the United States." Also during the 1940s, the

Delaware River had one of the highest levels of chemical contaminants in fish and shellfish in America. In fact, untreated human sewage and chemical factory wastes had contaminated the river so badly that no fish could survive in its oxygen-weakened waters. In the 1940s and 50s, excess nutrients caused the river to become totally devoid of oxygen for a 20-mile stretch in the Philadelphia/Camden area. As a result, fish such as American shad couldn't migrate upriver to their spawning grounds, they had to turn back or be suffocated. In addition, because of past pollution problems, portions of the estuary presently have bans or advisories on consumption of finfish due to polychlorinated biphenyl (PCB) concentrations.

In order to save and replenish the American shad, an effort in the 1960s began that reestablished the population of shad in the Delaware River Basin. That is when pollution levels in the basin declined significantly when fish ladders were built. These ladders allowed the shad to bypass the dams that blocked their way and to migrate further up the river.

Over the years, many efforts were undertaken to clean up the Delaware River but with little impact. Yet fortunately in 1962, the Delaware River Basin Commission was formed and joined the efforts of New York, New Jersey, Pennsylvania, and Delaware to restore the health of the river. In 1972, the Commission received $1 billion in federal grants under the Water Pollution Control Act. This Water Act improved the Delaware's nutrient problem, reduced pollution and finally the river began its exciting comeback.

Philadelphia recently helped the annual migration of the American shad; the city now sees the bony fish as a symbol of hope for its formerly polluted waterways. Every spring, the Delaware and the Schuylkill rivers close to Philadelphia used to run dense with spawning shad. Thus for many ears, pollution depleted parts of the waterways of oxygen, making a barrier to the fish's annual migration. However, in the decades since the Clean Water Act, which was developed in 1972, the cleanliness of the Delaware and Schuylkill has made a huge comeback.

The Delaware River has seen a promising resurgence of shad but the Schuylkill River remains vacant due to dams constructed along the waterway. Fortunately, Philadelphia's Fish and Boat Commission is restoring the shad to its native habitat by constructing fish ladders, in which fish swim upstream over a series of wooden steps. The six-feet-per-second current is fast enough to offer resistance but does not overpower them. In addition, there is a platform inside the ladder where the fish can rest.

Another factor contributing to the Delaware River's cleanliness comeback is the 2007-2012 recession, which drastically reduced production in plants located along the river. Prior to the recession, DuPont Company's Edge Moor Pigment Plant in east Wilmington, Delaware was once our country's leading source of highly toxic byproducts.

In 2009, the Environmental Protection Agency (EPA) reported a 45 percent, one-year drop in the amount of dioxins and related wastes generated by the DuPont Company's Edge Moor Plant in East Wilmington.

Also emissions moved downward at other sites as well in 2008, including at New Castle County, Delaware's now-idled automobile plants and the shuttered Dow Reichhold Specialty Latex Plant near Dover, Delaware. Environmentalists hope that reductions in pollution are signs of a move to a greener economy.

The good news is through efforts from federal, state, local and private agencies within the past several decades, many aspects of water quality have been enhanced within the Delaware River (a major river system of the Northeast). In fact, numerous aspects of water quality have also improved in other major river systems in the northeast that include New York's Hudson River, the Connecticut River in Conn. and Maine's Penobscot River.

Although the efforts and results of the Delaware River cleanup are a victory for clean waterways, the pollution issue has not gone away. Despite the economic downturn, some local plants are still nationally significant for their emissions. For example, Formosa Plastics, Inc. located near Delaware City was America's top source of toxic vinyl chloride air pollution in 2007. The company's emissions also increased by a third in 2008. In addition to Formosa Plastics, DuPont's big Chambers Works site in New Jersey near the Delaware Memorial Bridge increased its chemical releases to the Delaware River by twenty percent during 2007, when the company ranked as the nation's sixth-highest source of toxic pollution to water.

Furthermore, even though the water quality of the Delaware has improved compared to what it encountered decades ago, the waters in the Philadelphia, Pennsylvania/Camden, New Jersey Metropolitan Area still don't support fishing and swimming. In addition, new and unforeseen pollution threats (urban and agricultural runoff and abandoned mine drainage) are now arising for the Delaware River, Hudson River, and other rivers in North America.

Moreover, while the water in the Delaware River is relatively clean, the decades of industrial pollution have left a legacy in the river bottom. Pollutants like PCBs, lead, mercury (which restricts fish consumption), DDT, and other pesticides still remain in river-bottom detritus. Highest sediment PCB concentrations occurred adjacent to urbanized and industrialized reaches of the estuary. Scientists also found some PCB concentrations on bottom-feeding fish such as white perch and channel catfish. Invertebrates, such as zooplankton and scuds, feed on river-bottom detritus and ingest the pollutants. Then these pollutants work up the food chain and are concentrated in other fish and fish predators: black bears, bald eagles, and humans.

Other pollution threats to the river are ongoing. During storms, pollution from the land in the basin is washed into the river. This includes pesticides and herbicides, fertilizers, and mine tailings. The most damaging is called point-source pollution. These direct discharges come from factories, sewage treatment plants, power and chemical plants, paper mills, and refineries.

The Delaware Water Gap Area (Middle Delaware) is a part of Pennsylvania that experiences acid precipitation. This "acid rain" affects all watersheds in this section of Pennsylvania. Acid Rain also limits the river's fish community and aquatic life. During the 1960s, is when scientists and the general public began noticing that acid rain affected fish and aquatic organism populations in the Delaware. Due to acid rain, trees that bordered the Delaware and other rivers were also dying. Scientists also claim that factory and automobile pollution is poisoning the water in lakes and rivers.

Oil is another pollutant that severely affected the Delaware River. On November 26, 2004, the Athos I, a huge cargo vessel, struck a submerged anchor while preparing to dock in Paulsboro, New Jersey. The anchor punctured the hull, spilling almost 265,000 gallons of crude oil into the Delaware River. This oil spill resulted in damage to more than 280 miles of coastline, affecting aquatic organisms, habitats, fish, birds and other wildlife, as well as impeding recreational use of the river.

Another oil spill occurred in June 1989 when the Tanker *Presidente Rivera* spilled an estimated hundred thousand to million gallons of oil into the river. The oil greatly poisoned the river's water quality resulting in the infection and death of many fish, birds, and other wildlife in the region.

Toxic pollution is another potential threat to the water quality of the Delaware Estuary. In 1997, the state of New Jersey discharged 3,696,975 pounds (toxic chemical release to water) of chemicals into the river. Delaware dumped 490,419 pounds into the Delaware Estuary whereas Pennsylvania released 190,815 pounds of toxic chemicals into the river.

The company polluter that discharged the largest amounts of toxic chemicals into the Delaware in 1997 was Du Pont Chemical Company. In fact, Du Pont's Deepwater, New Jersey plant discharged 3,086,517 pounds of toxic chemicals into the river. In addition, a Du Pont plant in Gibbstown, NJ released 410,074 pounds into the Delaware Estuary.

Another chemical company, Ciba Specialty Chemicals Corporation, dumped 185,302 pounds from its Newport, Delaware plant into the river. Moreover, Allied-Signal Inc. dumped 107,022 pounds from its Philadelphia, PA facility into the Delaware River.

The year 1997 was indeed a disastrous one regarding pollution, which negatively affected the health of the Delaware River. The U.S. Public Interest Research Group (PIRG), an organization that interpreted data compiled from the U.S. Environmental protection Agency, stated that of all U.S. rivers, the Delaware River in 1997 received the biggest amount of carcinogen (an agent producing or inciting cancer) releases.

Compared to the 1990s and many decades prior to that period, the condition and water quality of the Delaware River today is much better. Once foul smelling and oxygen starved along its tidal reach downriver of Trenton, New Jersey, the Delaware River, from its headwaters in New York's Catskill Mountains to the Delaware Bay, now supports year-round fish populations, offering excellent bass, trout, walleye, striper, shad, and herring fisheries. Today, the Delaware River is one of the cleanest rivers in America. In fact, pleasure-craft marinas now line waterfronts once visited only by operators of commercial ships. Furthermore, attractive parks and greenways border the river and many of its tributaries. And not all businesses on the Delaware have neglected the river's health and environment. In fact, one in particular, Campbell's Soup, Inc., has helped to keep the environment clean in and around the Delaware River. Campbell's is a landmark on the Delaware River and in Camden, New Jersey and remarkably, Camden has been the company's home since 1869. Moreover, in order to help protect the Delaware River's environment, the company is currently reducing greenhouse gas emissions and improving water quality by using fertilizer more effectively and improving soil conservation in its wheat sourcing areas.

Although the Delaware is much cleaner now than it was about forty years ago, pollution problems still plague the river. For example, environmentalists indicated that many times within the last 5 years, the Gilbert Power Plant (that uses natural gas or oil to generate electricity) in Holland Township, New Jersey has polluted the Delaware River and the air circulating around it. Environmentalists also claim they are concerned about the combustion process as a result of the Gilbert Generating Station that can produce acid rain and ozone particles throughout the entire state of New Jersey. In addition to the Gilbert Power Plant, other pollution problems that the Delaware now faces include toxics that include PCBs, dioxins, mercury, chlorinated pesticides, and chlorinated benzenes that contaminate the food chain and fish. Due to toxic contaminants, the Delaware Estuary states, New Jersey, Pennsylvania, and Delaware have all issued advisories for fish consumption. Many fish such as channel catfish, striped bass, American eel, white perch, and white sucker are subject to no-eat fish advisories in numerous parts of the estuary. People also have been advised that consumption of other fish (largemouth bass, chain pickerel, and bluefish) should only be eaten in limited quantities.

But despite the present pollution threats, government programs are currently in place to protect the Delaware Estuary's water quality and address problems that still remain on the river. The potential pollution problems that continue to plague the Delaware Estuary consist of the river's lower reaches, which are bordered by heavy industry and the fact that the second biggest oil-refining petrochemical center in America lies on the bank of the Delaware River. It is vital that these government programs are

Photo taken in 1925 of Campbell's Soup Company on the Delaware near the Ben Franklin Bridge (joins Camden, N.J. with Philadelphia, Pa.)

Courtesy of Campbell's Soup, Inc.

In the foreground is the Delaware River. Directly behind the Delaware is the Gilbert Power Plant in Holland Township, New Jersey, which was built in 1928.

Photo by Stephen Harris.

successful to achieve both a healthy environment and economic vitality within the Delaware River Region.

For about the past forty years, the Delaware River Basin Commission, a pioneer organization in environmental protection, has joined other government agencies and private firms to clean up the Delaware and its feeder streams. Industry and business also have helped out with the river cleanup.

Regarding river clean up, each summer there is a Delaware River Cleanup Day where individuals and groups help clean up the estuary. Kittatinny Canoes formed the first river clean up event in 1990. The cleanup has become an annual tradition for many people who appreciate and care for the Delaware River. After the June 2006 flood, the canoe liveries and the Delaware Water Gap National Recreation Area joined together to sponsor an annual, one-day, volunteer clean-up effort. Since 2006, volunteers have removed 89 tons of garbage from the river.

In 2009, the Commission also made a significant determination regarding the regulation of natural gas projects in the Delaware River Watershed. Natural gas drilling will occur mainly in the Upper and Middle Delaware River Areas in Pennsylvania and New York. Projections show that the richest deposits of shale gas may be under Wayne County in Pennsylvania and Delaware and Sullivan Counties in New York.

The Delaware River Basin Commission recently announced that natural gas drillers must apply and receive the Commission's approval before starting any gas extraction project in shale formations that are located in Special protection Waters. This applies to water withdrawals, gas wells, and discharges of wastewater related to all shale gas projects. In addition, all kinds of gas drilling will be reviewed by the Commission and on site pits for potential direct and nonpoint source pollution impacts.

Moreover, the Delaware River Basin Commission started a toxic management program over ten years ago. The commission recently took a significant step to ensure that water quality standards for certain toxic pollutants in the tidal Delaware are met as part of its ongoing program to protect aquatic species and human health. Thanks to the commission and other agencies, the Delaware River now is the cleanest it's been in a hundred years.

In addition to the Commission's efforts to prevent, limit, and/or eliminate toxic pollution in the Delaware River, the

Environmental Protection Agency (EPA) recently presented measures to help prevent and resolve ship pollution problems. Today, pollution from ships' smokestacks remains a threat to the water quality of the Delaware River, Hudson River, and other large American rivers.

Specifically, in 2009, the EPA proposed new regulations on smokestack pollution from ships, demanding lower-sulfur fuel and more efficient engines from the maritime industry. The rules, which would likely go into effect in 2012, would decrease sulfur in marine fuel by 96 percent, slash emissions from smokestacks by 85 percent, and reduce smog-causing nitrogen oxide by 80 percent.

Although the Delaware River is now the cleanest it has ever been for the past ten decades, a huge issue that river advocates and the river itself must face is dredging. For many years, a lot of residents and officials have supported dredging while numerous citizens and environmentalists have opposed it.

When it comes to dredging, most people employed by the marine industry think dredging the Delaware River will have a positive impact to the environment and the economy. Marine professionals have clearly said that deepening the Delaware River an extra five feet can help to rid the PCB levels as well as give a positive boost to the economy.

In addition to those employed by the marine industry, Pennsylvania Governor Edward G. Rendell supported a 2008 agreement between the U.S. Army Corps of Engineers and the Philadelphia Regional Port Authority (PRPA) to deepen the Delaware River's shipping channel. This agreement allows the U.S. Army Corps of Engineers, in partnership with the PRPA, to increase by five feet the current forty-foot depth of the river's shipping channel from Camden's Beckett Street Terminal to the mouth of the Delaware Bay (a length of 102 miles). Governor Rendell said the agreement would expand commerce and enhance economic development in the area.

However, environmentalists and concerned citizens oppose the U.S. Army Corps of Engineers/PRPA dredging plan. They argue that deepening the Delaware will come at great cost to the aquatic plants, aquatic animals, other wildlife, and even people who live along the river. Opponents state that according to the proposed project, the Army Corps of Engineers will dredge about

33 million cubic yards of river sediment, much of it contaminated with mercury, lead, and PCBs.

In addition, many residents and environmentalists argue that blasting operations may damage the rock bed that protects a pristine aquifer now serving Delaware, Pennsylvania, and New Jersey. In addition, groups against the dredging project mentioned that most refineries have not committed to deepening their private "approach channels," that would be needed to accommodate the bigger ships and take advantage of the deepened channel. Those against dredging also mentioned that the project threatens to harm Delaware River water quality, wetlands, and nearby drinking water supplies.

Finally, opponents to the dredging plan believe that the project will mostly benefit oil refineries along the river, none of which have pledged financial support for the dredging plan. Many people against the plan say dredging the Delaware will also not produce any significant financial benefit to the surrounding communities.

Digressing to the improved condition of the Delaware River, many pollution threats still remain that have the potential to negatively impact the health of the river. Case in point, it will take a group effort to address and resolve these pollution threats to the river.

In the Delaware River's upper portion, the East and West Branches of the river are currently impounded by reservoirs that feed the New York City water supply system. This particular water system has an adverse impact on the river's water quality. About one third of the headwaters flow of the Delaware is diverted to the City of New York and consumed out of the watershed, depriving the Delaware River of fresh water volume. Furthermore, the reservoirs act as pollutant sinks and end up adding degraded water to the Upper Basin through releases into the river. Specifically, the Cannonsville Reservoir in Delaware County, New York negatively impacts the Upper Delaware River's water quality.

In 2007, the Upper Delaware River in New York was unfortunately ranked in fourth place as one of America's most endangered rivers due to a threat of a proposed power line. Fortunately, plans by New York Regional Interconnect, a private power company, to build a power line that would cut through the

Wild and Scenic portion of the Upper Delaware were killed in 2008.

However, the Energy Policy Act of 2005(the same act that could have permitted the power line project) exempts the gas and oil industries from the Safe Drinking Water Act in their extraction of methane from the Marcellus Shale Formation. Marcellus Shale is a gigantic natural gas seam that extends from New York through West Virginia and underlies most of the Delaware River Watershed. Many drilling leases have recently been signed and others are in progress. New York City Council is calling for a ban on this practice that threatens the drinking water supply for over 23 million Americans who depend on the Upper Delaware Watershed for clean drinking water.

Yet despite different pollution threats, residents, businesses, local, state, and federal officials, and environmentalists must continue working together by educating the public about how water pollution can devastatingly affect many communities. Many groups, citizens, and agencies must also implement preventive measures, enforce strict environmental laws, and organize cleanup efforts on a daily, weekly, and monthly basis to ensure that the Delaware River will remain relatively clean for the next hundred years.

Although progress has been made toward the condition of the Delaware, controlling pollutants and keeping the water relatively clean in the Delaware River Basin are not the only continuous concerns for wildlife officials, scientists, and residents. Today, global warming and climate change are raising concerns for the Delaware River Basin especially for the Lower Delaware River and Delaware Bay shorelines vulnerable to sea level changes and wetland losses. In fact, in 2010, a study of rising temperatures of American rivers conducted by ecologists and hydrologists in Maryland indicated that the longest record of temperature increase was observed for the Hudson River at Poughkeepsie, New York and the most rapid rate of temperature increase was recorded for the Delaware River near Chester, Pennsylvania.

In addition to climate change and rising river temperatures, Delaware River Basin Commission (DRBC) officials stated that the condition of the river, tributaries and watershed is "fair" although serious problems remain, ranging from flood control to threatened species (includes oysters, freshwater mussels, Atlantic sturgeon and brook trout) to habitat loss.

After decades of recovery and protection efforts, researchers rated over two-thirds of 37 environmental indicators as good or fair, including water supplies, water flows and oxygen levels in river water that once suffocated fish and other aquatic life. However, researchers estimated that rising water levels could submerge giant tracts of wetlands over time; eliminating areas that now hold back flooding and filter out contaminants from waterways.

A DRBC report also stated that salinity levels could increase along the river as increasing sea levels push salt water farther upriver especially during the summer. About 15 million people in four states live within the Delaware's complex watershed. Hence, communities with drinking water intakes along the river could be at risk, including Philadelphia, a city of more than 1 million people, and residents of New York City also intake drinking water from a branch of the Delaware River.

Moreover, higher water levels and warmer temperatures are likely to alter natural habitats and increase flooding and drought. Wildlife officials and scientists said that flooding already is a big concern, along with widespread warnings against eating some kinds of fish contaminated with pollutants, threats to some bird and aquatic species, and continued loss of habitat to development.

DRBC officials also mentioned that river basin groups are concerned about new kinds of toxic pollutants (flame-retardant and toxic chemicals and pesticides) and their effect on ecosystems. Researchers and scientists also want to make better systems for evaluating and tracking the health of the watershed and potential consequences of climate change.

In addition to flood control, threatened species, and climate change, one of the biggest threats to the Delaware lies on the way the river flows. About 50 percent of the Delaware's headwaters is diverted to New York City's municipal water supply system, and never returns to the watershed. The withdrawals and releases that cause this diversion make big changes in the natural flow of the river. This natural flow consists of periodic changes of water level, volume, scouring and flooding that make the habitats upon which the Delaware River's life depends. These flow alterations threaten the survival of freshwater animals like crayfish, mussels and amphibians. Changes to the river's flow also affect the health of the whole Delaware River system.

Moreover, changes in land use along the river's banks cause dramatic changes in the way the water runs. The river's floodplains are rich stores of biodiversity, and serve as crucial natural regulators of the water coursing down the river. Their thickly accumulated soils and dense floodplain forest slow the path of seasonal floods and help absorb the impact of storm events. However, the Delaware's floodplains have seen heavy development, and fewer are left to calm the river's rush. Recent years have seen mass destruction from repeated heavy floods in the middle and lower portions of the river.

Within the Upper Delaware, gas drilling is a pollution threat to that portion of the river. The Upper Delaware provides drinking water for about 17 million people throughout New York and Pennsylvania. Yet despite gas and unfavorable impacts to water quality caused by reservoirs and increasing development, the quality of water in the Upper Delaware remains relatively good. In fact, it's so good that the upper section of the Delaware has been designated by the Delaware River Basin Commission as Special Protection Waters and is entitled to more regulatory protections. Meanwhile, overland pollutant transport via surface runoff and flooding is a primary concern in the management of agricultural land resources in the Delaware River Basin. And although there are continuous threats and concerns that could negatively affect the condition of the Delaware River, overall, the Delaware River Basin has seen spectacular improvements to its water quality that it hasn't seen in decades!

Indeed, a clean and healthy Delaware River also stimulates the economy. When the Delaware River is in good condition, it boosts jobs, tourism, commercial fisheries, property values and tax bases. The health of the Delaware becomes even more critical during tough economic times.

In fact, in 2010, economic reports generated from the Delaware Riverkeeper indicated that in only one year, the Upper Delaware River and Delaware Water Gap attracted 367,4000 whitewater paddlers who spent over $20 million and supported 447 jobs. Riverkeeper reports also indicate that Delaware River festivals draw about 75,000 tourists to small riverside towns, giving a significant boost to local businesses. Furthermore, trout fishing in the Upper Delaware created $17.69 million in local business revenue, supporting 348 jobs while providing $3.65 million in wages and $719,350 in local taxes.

Chapter 3
Crossings (Bridges) of the Delaware River

There are many bridges that help motorists and railroads cross the Delaware River. Whether you need to cross the river to get from New Jersey to Pennsylvania, from Pennsylvania to New York or from Delaware to New Jersey, there are spans that will guide you to your state of choice. In this chapter I will describe many of the most popular bridges that many people have traveled on to go over the Delaware River to end up at their destination.

One of the most well-known Delaware River bridges that connect Pennsylvania and New Jersey is the Lower Trenton Bridge. This span is a 2-lane through truss bridge that extends over the Delaware River between Trenton, New Jersey and Morrisville, Pennsylvania. The Trenton Bridge is also known as the Trenton Makes Bridge because of its large lettering on the south side reading "TRENTON MAKES THE WORLD TAKES," installed in 1935. In addition to being a significant bridge from Pennsylvania to New Jersey, it is a major landmark in the city of Trenton.

As one goes down river, this bridge is the last free vehicular crossing of the Delaware. Although the Delaware River Joint Toll Bridge Commission (DRJTBC) owns it, no toll is collected. Historically, the Lower Trenton Bridge was originally a toll bridge operated by the Trenton Delaware Bridge Company. It opened on January 30, 1806, and was the first bridge across the Delaware River. In 1935, the "Trenton Makes The World Takes" sign on the south side of the bridge was installed and was first replaced in 1981. In 2005, the sign was replaced with one featuring higher-efficiency neon lighting, with better water proofing than the old sign, to help decrease maintenance costs.

Furthermore, the "Trenton Makes The World Takes" sign is now seen easily from Amtrak, New Jersey Transit, and other passenger railroads on the Northeast corridor as the trains cross the river. On northbound trains, the sign can be seen from the left side of the train, on southbound trains, from the right.

In regards to the Delaware's tides and the bridge's location, the "Trenton Makes" Bridge crossing the Delaware at Morrisville is at the upper most stretches of the Atlantic Ocean tide. Just up river from the bridge there is a little noticeable change in tide. But down river from the span the tide rises and drops twice a day, and these changes can be quite huge. Large rocks and boulders seen in the river between the "Trenton Makes" Bridge (Lower Bridge) and the Calhoun Street Bridge (Upper Bridge that also connects Trenton, New Jersey with Morrisville, Pennsylvania) mark the edge of the Piedmont Plateau where it meets the coastal plain. In fact, this hard rock barrier is what stops the tide at this point. This area known as the Falls of the Delaware and from this point northward, the Delaware is a completely different river than the deeper tidal waters of the coastal plain. Here is where the river flows strong through some of the shallower rocky spots and then slows down a pinch in the deeper pools.

In addition to the Lower Trenton Bridge, there is the Trenton-Morrisville Toll Bridge that connects Trenton, New Jersey with Morrisville, Pennsylvania. This bridge, which opened in 1952, carries U.S. Route 1 and is operated by the Delaware River Joint Toll Bridge Commission. Today, tolls are collected only from motorists traveling southbound (entering Pennsylvania/departing New Jersey). The span's total length is 1,324 feet and its width is 62 feet.

Yet another Trenton Bridge that crosses the Delaware River is the Calhoun Street Toll Bridge. This is a historic bridge, with a vertical clearance of eight feet, a load limit of three short tons and a total length of 1,274 feet that connects Calhoun Street in Trenton New Jersey across the Delaware to East Trenton Avenue in Morrisville, Pennsylvania. The Calhoun Street Bridge is owned by the Delaware River Joint Toll Bridge Commission, and is maintained with tolls from other bridges.

The Phoenix Bridge Company of Phoenixville, Pennsylvania built the Calhoun Street Bridge in 1884. The bridge was part of the Lincoln Highway until 1920(when the highway was moved to the free Lower Trenton Bridge) and was later connected to Brunswick Circle by the Calhoun Street Extension as part of a bypass of downtown Trenton.

In addition to the Trenton Bridges, the Delaware Memorial Bridge is a very popular span that crosses the Delaware and a drive over the Delaware Memorial provides views of Wilmington, Delaware and distant Philadelphia, Pennsylvania. However, with the tops of the supporting structures over forty stories high, the bridge can be seen from the ground from many vantage points miles away.

The Delaware Memorial is a set of twin suspension, toll bridges that carry Interstate 295 and U.S. Route 40 between Delaware and New Jersey. This 2 and a half-mile-long bridge is one of only two crossings of the Delaware River with both U.S. highway and Interstate highway designations, the other being the Benjamin Franklin Bridge. Moreover, the two Delaware Memorial Bridges stand as the world's longest twin(side-by-side) suspension spans.

The bridges provide a vital regional connection for long-distance travelers. While not part of Interstate 95, they connect two parts of the highway: the Delaware Turnpike (Interstate 95 in Delaware) on the south side with the New Jersey Turnpike (later Interstate 95 in New Jersey) on the north side. These two bridges also connect Interstate 495, U.S. Route 13, and Route 9 in New Castle, Delaware with U.S. Route 130 in Pennsville Township, New Jersey (at the settlement of Deepwater, New Jersey).

The Delaware Memorial Bridge is dedicated to those from both Delaware and New Jersey who died in World War II, the Korean War, and the Vietnam War. On the Delaware side of the bridge is a War Memorial, visible from the northbound side lanes. The Delaware River and Bay Authority operate the toll facility.

Construction of the Delaware Memorial started in 1949. By 1951, a single-span suspension bridge with a road deck 175 feet high slowly rose above the Delaware River. The towering support structures, standing on either side of the Delaware River, climb 440 feet above the water. Opening with four lanes, the bridge handled traffic loads beyond projections. In 1955, 8 million cars drove over the Delaware Memorial Bridge. By 1960, 15 million motorists had used the bridge.

After 1960, the bridge was bombarded with millions of motorists each year. Fortunately, a second nearby bridge, which was nearly an identical span over the river, was built in 1968. The second span parallels the original bridge, making the Delaware Memorial Bridge a dual-span structure offering drivers eight lanes of roadway.

Besides the Delaware Memorial Bridge, there's another well-known span called the Benjamin Franklin Bridge. This bridge, originally named the Delaware River Bridge, is a suspension bridge across the Delaware joining Philadelphia, Pa.

with Camden, New Jersey. Named for American statesman Benjamin Franklin, the bridge is operated and owned by the Delaware River Port Authority.

The Ben Franklin Bridge now carries highways I-676 and US 30. It also accommodates the Port Authority Transit Corporation's Lindenwold High-Speed Line (PATCO Speedline) via connecting tunnels on both sides of the bridge.

Moreover, the bridge has seven vehicular lanes that are divided by a concrete "zipper" barrier that can be moved mechanically to configure the lanes for traffic volume or construction. Overhead red and green signals indicate which lanes are open or closed to traffic in each direction. Before the zipper barrier was installed, one lane of the bridge was kept closed at peak times to lower the risk of head-on collisions, as there was no physical barrier separating east and westbound traffic.

In addition, pedestrian walkways run along both sides of the bridge, elevated over and separated from the vehicular lanes; of this only one is open at a time. However, the Delaware River Port Authority closes the walkway after snowfall, a hurricane, and during security concerns. The 533-metre bridge span, which opened on July 1, 1926, is one of four main bridges (other bridges are the Walt Whitman, Betsy Ross, and Tacony-Palmyra) that connect Philadelphia with southern New Jersey.

Like the Ben Franklin Bridge, the Walt Whitman Bridge spans the Delaware River from Philadelphia to southern Jersey, specifically Gloucester City, New Jersey. The name of this bridge derived from the poet Walt Whitman, who lived in Camden, New Jersey toward the end of his life. The Walt Whitman Bridge is one of the biggest bridges on the eastern part of the United States. The span is owned and operated by the Delaware River Port Authority.

Walt Whitman is a bridge that represents part of Interstate 76(which, between the river and the Pennsylvania Turnpike interchange in King of Prussia, PA, is known as the "Schuylkill Expressway"). In addition to the Benjamin Franklin Bridge, Delaware Memorial Bridge, Betsy Ross Bridge, and Commodore Barry Bridge, the Walt Whitman is one of five expressway-standard bridges that connect Philadelphia with southern New Jersey.

The bridge has a total length of 11,981 feet and a main span of 2,000 feet. It also has seven lanes, three in each direction and a center lane that is shifted variably (via a zipper barrier) to hold heavy traffic when needed. Walt Whitman Bridge was built in 1953 and opened to traffic on May 16, 1957.

Another famous bridge span that crosses the Delaware is the Betsy Ross Bridge. Owned, operated, and maintained by the Delaware River Port Authority of Pennsylvania and New Jersey, Betsy Ross is a continuous steel truss bridge (its total length is 8,485 feet, longest span is 729 ft.) that crosses the Delaware River from Philadelphia to Pennsaukan, New Jersey. Betsy Ross connects New Jersey Route 90, which allows drivers to use NJ 90 to access Route 73, rather than via U.S. Route 130.

Betsy Ross Bridge was originally planned to open as the Delair Bridge, after a paralleling vertical lift bridge owned by the Pennsylvania Railroad (now used by Conrail and NJ Transit's Atlantic City Line), but instead was named for Betsy Ross, the creator of the first American flag. Hence, that makes the Betsy Ross Bridge only the second bridge in America to be named after a woman (after Iowa's Kate Shelley High Bridge in 1912).

Construction of the Betsy Ross Bridge started in 1969 but the bridge did not open until 1976 because of many problems with the communities where the bridge's ramps were located.

Besides the Betsy Ross Bridge, motorists will see yet another bridge, which one is called the Burlington-Bristol Bridge. The Burlington-Bristol Bridge is a steel bridge that comes with a lift span crossing the Delaware River from Burlington, New Jersey to Bristol Township, Pennsylvania.

The bridge, operated by the Burlington County Bridge Commission, carries two lanes of traffic (PA 413 and NJ 413) and has a total length of 2,301 feet. Burlington-Bristol is a main route to Philadelphia for the area's residents and normally preferred to the other bridges by bus drivers since the tolls are lower. The width of the bridge is 20 feet and its clearance for boats is 135 feet.

Building the Burlington-Bristol Bridge began on April 1, 1930 and the bridge opened to traffic on May 1, 1931, after only thirteen months of construction. When the bridge opened, motorists paid just 35 cents to cross the span.

Another bridge that crosses the Delaware River is the Tacony-Palmyra Bridge. Tacony-Palmyra is a double-leaf bascule, steel arch bridge that crosses the Delaware, connecting Route 73 in Palmyra, New Jersey and Route 73 in the Tacony section of

Philadelphia, Pennsylvania. The bridge, owned and maintained by the Burlington County Bridge Commission, is 38 feet wide, has a total length of 3,659 feet and spans 2,324 feet.

A Polish architect named Ralph Modjeski originally designed Tacony-Palmyra. After one and a half years of construction, it opened on August 14, 1929 to replace the local ferry service. Although it first opened as a 4-lane bridge, the lanes were reduced in a 1996-97-bridge deck-replacement project to three wider lanes. These lanes now consist of two toll lanes northwestward into Philadelphia, and one free lane southeastward into New Jersey.

In addition to Tacony-Palmyra, there is the Commodore Barry Bridge. Commodore Barry is one of four toll bridges that connect the Philadelphia region with southern New Jersey and it carries five lanes (US 322 and CR 536(NJ) and two lanes of sidewalk). Commodore Barry is a cantilever bridge that spans the Delaware River from Chester, Pennsylvania to Bridgeport, in Logan Township, New Jersey. It is named after John Barry; Barry lived in Philadelphia and is an American Revolutionary War hero.

Workers started to build the bridge on April 14, 1969 and it opened to traffic on February 1, 1974. Commodore Barry is 77 feet wide, its clearance is 192 feet, has a main span of 1,644 feet and a total length of 13,912 feet, making it the longest bridge in the United States and the fourth-longest cantilever bridge in the world.

Moving on to another bridge there is the New Hope-Lambertville Bridge. This bridge, officially named the New Hope-Lambertville Toll Supported Bridge, is a 6-span, 23 foot-wide, 1,053-foot-long bridge spanning the Delaware River that joins the city of Lambertville in Hunterdon County, New Jersey with the borough of New Hope in Bucks County, Pennsylvania. Today, it is maintained and owned as a toll-free span by the Delaware River Joint Toll Bridge (DRJTB) Commission.

Compared to other spans that cross the Delaware, the current New Hope-Lambertville Toll Supported Bridge has three unique characteristics. One, more pedestrians use the bridge than any other span along the whole length of the Delaware River. Two, the walkway is cantilevered off the bridge's downstream side. It consists of fiberglass panels, the only walkway of its type in the DRJTB system. Finally, the bridge has a sewer line attached to its upstream side. The forced sewer main is owned by the Bucks

County Water and Sewer Authority and carries sewage from New Hope across the river to Lambertville and to the treatment plant operated by the Lambertville Municipal Utilities Authority.

The original 1,051-foot-long and 32-foot-wide wooden covered bridge was constructed on September 12, 1814. However, the flood of 1841 heavily damaged the original bridge. A second wooden bridge was erected in 1842 but was destroyed during the flood of 1903. So as was the case with many of the Delaware River bridges at that time, that flood and other floods encouraged replacing the wooden structure with a modern steel bridge. Thus with a vertical clearance of 13 feet, the structure, New Hope-Lambertville Bridge, dates back to 1904 when its steel truss spans were originally built.

Yet another popular Delaware River span is the Uhlerstown-Frenchtown Bridge. This is a free bridge that crosses over the Delaware and is owned and operated by the Delaware River Joint Toll Bridge Commission. The span carries Bridge Street, connecting New Jersey Route 12 in Frenchtown, and Hunterdon County, New Jersey with Pennsylvania Route 32 (River Road) in Uhlerstown located in Bucks County, Pennsylvania. This bridge has a roadway width of 16 feet 6 inches and a pedestrian walkway that is supported on steel cantilever brackets.

The first bridge connecting Uhlerstown and Frenchtown was a six span, wooden, covered bridge erected upon five stone and masonry piers and two abutments. The six spans totaled over 1,000 feet in length and the Uhlerstown-Frenchtown Bridge was completed in about one year, at a cost of $20,000, and opened in the beginning of 1844.

Not far from Philadelphia is another bridge that crosses the Delaware called the Northampton Street Bridge. Northampton Street Bridge is a span connecting Easton, Pennsylvania and Phillipsburg, New Jersey. Although it is not a toll bridge, the Northampton Street Bridge is maintained by the Delaware River Joint Toll Bridge Commission. Locally, it is known as the "Free Bridge" distinguishing it from the Easton-Phillipsburg Toll Bridge just up the river to the north. Today, the steel bridge has a sidewalk decking, pedestrian railings, and is posted for a 3-ton weight limit with a 15 mile-per-hour speed limit.

In 1739, Northampton Bridge was originally a ferry crossing and the first wooden bridge was opened in 1806. The original bridge was designed and built by Timothy Palmer, one of the most famous bridge builders of his time. While other bridges fell during many floods and storms, Palmer's covered bridges remained standing. Another bridge that crosses the Lower Delaware is the Washington Crossing Bridge. Constructed in 1904 by the Taylorsville Delaware Bridge Company, this truss span connects Titusville in Mercer County, New Jersey with Washington Crossing in Bucks County, Pennsylvania.

Now owned and operated by the Delaware River Joint Toll Bridge Commission, Washington Crossing Bridge is an 877-foot-long, six-span double truss structure. Its riveted-steel grid deck provides motorists with a 15-foot-wide roadway that is made of a grate. The bridge's substructures, made of rubble stone-faced masonry, are from the original 1831 bridge, while its superstructure dates to 1904. Five piers and two abutments support Washington Crossing and the bridge's south (downriver) side supports a cantilevered, wood planked pedestrian sidewalk that was added in 1926.

After leaving Bucks County, Pennsylvania, motorists will find yet another Delaware River crossing, which is the Delaware Water Gap Toll Bridge. This steel cable beam bridge, which carries four lanes of I-80 and the Appalachian Trail, is also known as the Interstate 80 Toll Bridge. The structure also has a pedestrian sidewalk on the south side of the New Jersey-bound section of the bridge, separated from motor vehicles with a concrete divider. The toll bridge carries Interstate 80 across the Delaware River at the Delaware Water Gap, connecting Hardwick Township, New Jersey and the Delaware Water Gap in Pennsylvania. The 28-foot wide, 2,465 foot-long bridge, built by the Delaware River Joint Toll Bridge Commission, is a multiple span dual roadway with a steel plate structure.

The Delaware Water Gap Bridge first opened to traffic on December 16, 1953 at ceremonies attended by New Jersey Governor Alfred E. Driscoll and Pennsylvania Governor John S. Fine. The bridge carried US 611(today it's Pennsylvania Route 611) for four miles in New Jersey to a connection with Route 94. Then a few years later in 1959, Interstate 80 was routed onto the bridge.

North of the Delaware Water Gap Bridge and Interstate 80 is where motorists will find the Dingman's Ferry Bridge. Today, this 530-foot-long, 18-foot wide, bridge that comes with a vertical clearance of 11 feet, represents an important link for commuters to reach destinations in New Jersey and New York City.

Opened in 1900, the Dingman's Ferry Bridge is the last privately owned toll bridge on the Delaware River and one of the last few in America. The bridge is owned and operated by the Dingmans Choice and Delaware Bridge Company. Hence, since he Bridge Company is fully responsible for its own repairs, it employs an engineering company (certified for bridge inspection) to regularly inspect the bridge from the tops of the trusses to the underwater foundations. Every September, the private bridge company closes the bridge the second week after Labor Day to conduct any repairs necessary to maintain the bridge's structure.

Dingman's Ferry Bridge was originally named after Dingman's Ferry in 1735 when Andrew Dingman, a Dutch pioneer from Kinderhook, New York, operated a ferry that connected the Old Mine Road in Sussex County, New Jersey to the Bethany Turnpike (today it's State Route 2019) in Delaware Township in Pike County, Pa.

In addition to the Dingman's Ferry Bridge, there's the Mid-Delaware Bridge. The Mid-Delaware Bridge, also known as the Fourth Barrett Bridge or Port Jervis-Matamoras Bridge, is a continuous steel truss bridge that carries US Routes 6 and 209 across the Delaware River between Port Jervis, New York and Matamoras, Pennsylvania.

The bridge, which now has a clearance below of 25 feet, a total length of 659 feet, and a width of 44 feet, is the only four-lane bridge on the upper primary stem of the Delaware River. As for its history, at a cost of $380,000, Ritz Construction Company constructed the Mid-Delaware Bridge in 1939. Today, the Joint Interstate Bridge Commission maintains the span.

Besides the Mid-Delaware Bridge, another span that crosses the Delaware and connects New York between Pennsylvania is the Narrowsburg-Darbytown Bridge. This two-lane bridge connects Darbytown, Pennsylvania with Narrowsburg, New York.

The bridge now carries two lanes of Pennsylvania Route 652 and New York Route 52. The Narrowsburg-Darbytown Bridge was finished and opened to traffic in 1953. The interstate bridge did not become toll free until January 12, 1927 when the New

York-Pennsylvania Joint Bridge Commission bought it at a cost of $55,000.

In Delhi, New York, motorists can access the Fitches Covered Bridge. This span is a historical wooden covered bridge standing in East Delhi (Delaware County), New York. Fitches Bridge carries Fitches Bridge Road over the West Branch of the Delaware River. This bridge is a 100-foot long, Town Lattice Truss crossing and was first constructed in 1870.

Another historical covered bridge in Delhi, New York is the Hamden Bridge. This bridge stands six miles southwest of Delhi in Delaware County, New York. Hamden Bridge supports Basin Clove Road over the West Branch of the Delaware River. It is a Long Truss with a span of 125 feet. The bridge was originally built in 1859.

Besides crossing the West Branch of the Delaware River, motorists can also cross the Delaware River's East Branch by driving on Bridge Street via Downsville Bridge. Like the old covered bridges in Delhi, New York, Downsville, built in 1854, is a historical covered bridge. This bridge, located in Downsville (Delaware County), New York, is a 174-foot span, has a vertical clearance of six feet, and has a Long with Queenpost Truss.

Finally, there's the Roebling Delaware Aqueduct. Although it doesn't exist today, the Roebling Delaware Aqueduct was the oldest existing wire cable suspension bridge in America. This bridge was erected and opened in 1848 as one of the major improvements on the Delaware and Hudson (D and H) Canal (1828-1898). The Delaware Aqueduct Bridge continued to be used as a private toll bridge until 1918.

Lower Trenton Bridge that spans over the Delaware connecting Trenton, New Jersey with Morrisville, Pennsylvania.

Photo taken by Ron Saari. Courtesy of the Delaware River Joint Toll Bridge Commission. The bridge and sign are owned and operated by the Delaware River Joint Toll Bridge Commission.

The Uhlerstown-Frenchtown Bridge crosses the Delaware River and connects Uhlerstown, Pennsylvania with Frenchtown, New Jersey.

This photo was taken by G. W. Freeland sometime between 1905 and 1910. Freeland took this photo from the southern end of the Frenchtown Railroad Station platform.

Chapter 4
Trails (Water and Land), Greenways, Parks, Historic Attractions and Recreation on the Delaware River

When it comes to water trails, one popular one is the Delaware River Water Trail. This trail starts from the headwaters of the Delaware from Hancock, New York to the head of tide in Trenton, New Jersey and Morrisville, Pennsylvania.

This water trail covers 220 miles of the river's freshwater segment and includes information providing an overview of the river and its excellent resources and opportunities for recreation that includes boating and hiking.

In the state of New York, the West Branch Preserve is an ideal spot for hiking. The southern boundary of this 446-acre preserve is located at the West Branch of the Delaware River. To the north, the preserve extends to a mountain ridge 1,000 feet above the river valley where forests make up about 250 acres. Of these, about 200 acres were logged about 25 years ago, while the remaining 50 acres are thought to be at the location of a farm abandoned in the 1830s.

The site is located in the Town of Hamden, New York about ten miles west of Delhi. Once guests enter the preserve, they will see two trails. One is a 0.7-mile trail marked in blue markers with a moderate ascent while the other trail is 2 miles long marked in orange on an old logging road that has a steep climb. Experienced hikers should only climb this trail.

On the blue trail you will see trees such as pines and hemlocks and on the orange trail you will se trees like the red maple, sugar maple, oak, and beech. Meanwhile, in some parts of the woodland area, you might see deer and near the Delaware River you will find rare riverweed (an endangered plant species).

In addition to the Delaware River Water Trail, you will find another smaller trail in New York. This trail is called the Upper Delaware Scenic Byway. This trail roughly parallels the Upper Delaware River from Port Jervis in Orange County to Hancock in Delaware County where the majority of the route lies in Sullivan County, New York.

Port Jervis, New York is situated on the scenic Upper Delaware River where the states of New York, Pennsylvania and

New Jersey meet. Port Jervis is also along a main flyway for the American bald eagle.

Moreover, due to its location and waterways, which includes the mouth of the Neversink River (a tributary of the Delaware River), Port Jervis has been a longtime transportation hub. In regards to Orange County, it is the only county in New York located between two rivers, the Delaware on the west and the Hudson on the east. As for the Upper Delaware Byway, it is in an area full of rich history, picturesque scenery, communities both quaint and lively, and recreational opportunities.

The Delaware River not only forms the scenic background to this attractive area, but also the historic backdrop to today's land patterns and communities. Panoramic views across the river to Pennsylvania emphasize the important role neighboring towns across the border have played and continue to play in life on the byway corridor.

Besides trails and recreation, one historic attraction in the Upper Delaware River Region that is now quite a point of interest for visitors is the Fort Delaware Museum located in Narrowsburg, New York, known as the Eagle Capital of New York State. A tour of Fort Delaware Museum includes demonstrations of early settlers' craft making and lifestyles.

Fort Delaware represents Cushetunk, the first white settlement on the Upper Delaware River, in 1754 by the Delaware Company Pioneers. The first settlers were farmers who came mainly from Connecticut and were of English descent. A group of Connecticut men then created "The Delaware Company" and became proprietors.

The Delaware Company bought land from the Lenape Indians and the first deed was signed in 1754. The land purchased was a ten-mile strip along both sides of the Delaware River (would be situated today in New York and Pennsylvania).

Outside of trails and museums, Roxbury, New York is an attraction of interest all in itself. The headwaters of the Delaware River flow through rural Roxbury, winding past tree-lined streets and the stonewalls of Kirkside Park, an 11-acre park. This area was primarily known for its dairy farms, the number that declined drastically in the second half of the 20th century. After naturalist John Burroughs (1837-1921) wrote about his home here and the surrounding mountains, the region attracted the interest of city dwellers.

During the 19th-century, financier Jay Gould and his family, whose fortune was made in railroads and the Western Union Telegraph Company, developed Roxbury. The Gould generations used their money to erect community centers and churches that still stand today.

Speaking about money Gould made with railroads, tourists can also ride on a railroad along the Delaware River in New York. In fact, the historic Delaware Ulster (D and U) Railroad based in Arkville, New York, transports passengers through a constant changing landscape of rolling fields, magnificent mountains, pastoral farms and quaint villages. The train rolls through the Catskill Mountains, along the fresh, clean waters of the East Branch of the scenic Delaware River.

The Delaware Ulster (D and U) Railroad offers a regular schedule of excursions on certain days from May to October. Special event trains include Twilight on the Rails and the Rip Van Winkle Flyer dinner train, which provides a first-class ride experiencing the Golden Age of Railroading. And in October, the Annual Bellesyre Fall Festival is hosted on the exposition grounds of the D and U. this event features food, crafts, music and scenic train rides. Furthermore, the railroad station offers visitors an exhibit about the significant role played by the railroad in the area's development.

Another New York State attraction is Barryville, a town situated on the Delaware River. Over the years, Barryville has attracted celebrities that retreated there away from city life. In fact, Bette Davis, John F. Kennedy, Charles Linburgh and Paul Newman were some of the celebrities who visited the town.

Besides New York's trails and other attractions, a popular trail on the Delaware is a land trail called the Delaware River Heritage Trail. This Heritage Trail is located in the tidal portion of the river in both New Jersey and Pennsylvania. It is a walking and bicycling trail that links the river communities and provides the means to appreciate the river area's heritage. This trail begins from Trenton, New Jersey, continues south to Palmyra, New Jersey, crosses over to Philadelphia, and continues north to Morrisville, Pa. across from Trenton.

In addition to the Delaware River Heritage Trail, river lovers can discover the Tidal Delaware Water Trail. This water trail spans over fifty miles from the Trenton, New Jersey and Morrisville Pennsylvania portion to Marcus Hook (a borough in Delaware County, Pa.) including the Pennsylvania and New Jersey sides of the river. Sailors, boaters, and kayakers can "ride the tide" past historic sites, ecological treasures, and modern recreational opportunities along its course. This trail is a good way to see a different side of the region from the water.

This water trail is special in that it's mainly in an urban setting and small boat craft and paddlers share the Delaware River with huge cargo ships. The Tidal Delaware River Trail is also one of the few tidal trails in existence, which means users pay close attention to the direction of the tides to plan their trip.

Along with land and water trails on the Delaware there are greenways. In New Jersey, we have the East Coast Greenway. The East Coast Greenway covers 94 miles between New York and Pennsylvania. The Greenway passes through major urban areas that include Trenton, Princeton, New Brunswick, Newark, and Jersey City as well as quiet suburban settings and more rural landscapes. Greenway users can access the East Coast Greenway by utilizing the bike/pedestrian friendly Calhoun Street Bridge that crosses the Delaware River between New Jersey and Pennsylvania.

In central New Jersey, visitors will find the 70-mile Delaware and Raritan Canal State Park located along the Delaware and Raritan Canal (D and R Canal). Today, the D and R Park is used for kayaking, canoeing and fishing. A natural-surface trail within the park along the side of the canal, which was the tow path that mules used to tow barges on the canal before steam-powered barges, is now utilized for horseback riding, hiking, jogging, and bicycling. The D and R Canal Park is also a significant wildlife corridor connecting fields and forests. A recent bird survey taken in the park revealed 160 species of birds, about 90 of which nested in the park.

In addition to the park, the D and R Canal was constructed in the 1830s and served to connect the Delaware River with the Raritan River in central New Jersey. The canal attracts many history lovers as it showcases its wooden bridges, 19th-century bridge tender houses, cobblestone spillways, and hand-made, stone-arched culverts. The Delaware and Raritan Canal was a reliable means of transporting freight between Philadelphia, Pennsylvania and New York City, especially coal from coal fields in eastern Pennsylvania. Prior to the railroad industry, the D and R Canal allowed shippers to cut many miles off the route from the Pennsylvania coal fields, down the Delaware River, around Cape May, New Jersey, and up along the Atlantic Ocean coast to New York City. The primary section of the Delaware and Raritan Canal runs from Bordentown, New Jersey on the Delaware River to New Brunswick, New Jersey on the Raritan River. A feeder canal section stretches 22 miles northbound from Trenton, New Jersey, upriver along the east bank of the Delaware to Bull's Island near Frenchtown, an old, historic New Jersey town.

Bull's Island is part of Bull's Island Recreation Area that is close to Frenchtown on the Delaware. This Recreation Area is a natural area that comprises a portion of a small-forested land surrounded by the Delaware River and the Delaware and Raritan Canal. A trail along the canal's towpath reveals a lowland floodplain forest dominated by tulip poplar, sycamore and silver maple. Many rare plant species are found in the Bull's Island Recreation Area.

New Jersey is also the state where you can see High Point State Park. At 1,803 feet, this highest point in New Jersey provides scenic views of the Kittatinny Mountain Ridge as well as the neighboring states of Pennsylvania and New York.

Bordering the Delaware River and Valley on the east, spectacular hawk migrations can be seen from these ridges each autumn. Common ridge habitats include hardwood swamps, glacial lakes, upland forest, streams, and ridge top towns with endangered plant species. In addition, the many wetlands in High Point State Park that is home to numerous species including otters, beavers, bears and great blue herons.

In South New Jersey, riverfront redevelopment is also emerging. Four Class A office buildings will soon be erected on an existing business park known as Commerce Square. Commerce Square, which is also by the Route 130 corridor and the Burlington-Bristol Bridge into Pennsylvania, will offer something different than the traditional suburban office park that people see in other areas of southern New Jersey, especially in Mount Laurel and Moorestown.

Delaware River at Bull's Island, located on the New Jersey side of the Delaware River.

Photo taken by Michael Hogan.

According to Jay O'Donnell, manager of The O'Donnell Group (a Moorestown-based commercial realty services firm), this urban business park offers employees flexibility to commute to work via public transit, on foot or by car. "This project will create up to 1,000 jobs and boost redevelopment efforts in Burlington City and other towns along the Delaware River," O'Donnell said. Besides commercial redevelopment riverside projects surfacing in the state, New Jersey is home to the Delaware River Scenic Byway. The Byway, which runs along New Jersey Route 29 on the eastern side of the river, is another interesting area to see. This Byway offers great views of the Delaware and travels through historic riverside towns of Titusville, Lambertville, Stockton, Prallsville, and Raven Rock ending at the southern part of Frenchtown. There are also many historic stops on the Byway, including the site of the Prallsville Mills. The Prallsville Mills is a good example of how historic sites can remain an active asset to the community today, while preserving our country's history in relation to our natural resources, transportation development, technology, and economic growth.

Besides trails and parks, some other Delaware River Region Attractions in New Jersey include the Burlington County Prison Museum, Nothnagle Log Cabin, the Camden Children's Garden, the Old Barracks, New Jersey State Aquarium, Rockingham Historic Site, Walt Whitman House, Air Victory Museum, and Whitesbog Village.

The Burlington County Prison Museum is a National Historic Landmark located in Historic Mount Holly. The Burlington County Prison was designed by Robert Mills, one of America's first native-born and trained architects and was built in 1811. The prison was one of Mills' first designs as an architect and the interior vaulted ceilings of poured concrete, brick, and stone construction made the building fireproof. In fact, it was so well erected that the County Prison remained in use until 1965.

The Nothnagle Log Cabin is listed on the National Register of Historic Sites. Located in Gibbstown (Salem County), New Jersey, this cabin was constructed at about 1638 by Swedish or Finnish settlers and the oldest standing log cabin in North America.

Nothnagle Log Cabin is a great existing example of early log cabin construction. Upon a base of rock barely seen in the ground, the logs were placed horizontally around the base, building upward. Unlike other early 17th Century cabins, this cabin was originally made without metal nails. Instead, the builder used trunnel pins, also known as treenails. These pins are small wooden dowels, with one edge given a wide wedge shape to help it secure when hammered into place. In the back corner of the cabin is a brick fireplace believed to have been constructed from imported Swedish bricks transported to New Jersey by the builder himself.

    Situated in Camden, New Jersey, there is the Camden Children's Garden. The garden is located across the Delaware River from Philadelphia and is next to Battleship New Jersey. The Children's Garden is accessible by the Riverlink Ferry from Penn's Landing or the River Line train.

    This four-acre garden is geared toward children and families. It is a unique place to explore and find the natural world and provides horticultural experiences for imaginative and creative play.

    Another attraction in the Delaware River Region is called the Old Barracks. The Old Barracks is both a State and National Landmark situated in Trenton, New Jersey. Erected in 1758 by the Colony of New Jersey during the French and Indian War, the Old Barracks was a witness to the Battle of Trenton in 1776, the turning point of the American Revolution.

    Today, the Old Barracks functions as an educational center for Colonial and American history and is the last remaining building of its kind. The staff of the Old Barracks now coordinates daily tours of American colonial life. The Old Barracks also offers a weapon and artifact museum, as well as the gift shop. Each year, over 20,000 school children and thousands of people from all over the globe visit the Old Barracks, making it one of the most visited attractions in New Jersey and one of the most significant historic sites in America.

    Then when tourists head south from Trenton, they can discover the New Jersey State Aquarium in Camden, New Jersey. This State Aquarium is located on the scenic Delaware River waterfront overseeing the Philadelphia skyline. The Aquarium offers exciting, all-ages experiences that include over eighty exhibits with more than 5,000 fish and about 800 species of aquatic animals.

In Kingston, New Jersey, you can visit the Rockingham Historic Site. For nearly three months in 1783, Rockingham served as General George Washington's final Revolutionary War headquarters.

The original two rooms of Rockingham were constructed between 1702 and 1710. During the 1760s, Judge John Berrien enlarged the site into a grander home. The house and grounds are presently preserved as the temporary home of George and Martha Washington. Since 1896, Rockingham Historic Site has been physically relocated three times. Today, it hosts a fine collection of 18th century furnishings, a Children's Museum, and a Colonial kitchen garden.

Camden, New Jersey is also home to the Walt Whitman House. Today, the Walt Whitman House, a National Historic Landmark, gives us a close look into the life of the famous poet, drawing tourists from around the world. Whitman's personal belongings, original letters, the bed in which he died, and the death notice that was nailed to the front door were all preserved, including a collection of unique 19th-century photographs (includes the earliest image of Whitman in 1848). The Walt Whitman House is located at 328 Mickle Boulevard, between 3rd and 4th Streets in Camden. The Whitman House stands two blocks east of the Camden waterfront on the Delaware River.

For many people, the history of the Walt Whitman House is also interesting. In 1884, Whitman bought a 2-story house on Mickle Street for $1,750; it's also the only house he ever owned. He lived there until he died in 1892, at the age of 72.

Prior to living on Mickle Street, Whitman came to Camden years earlier, in 1873, and lived with his brother George on nearby Stevens Street. By that time, his reputation attracted the attention of the day's most prominent literary figures. Among them, Oscar Wilde and famous author Charles Dickens came to Camden to visit America's greatest poet. When his brother George and his wife Louisa moved to Burlington, New Jersey, Walt chose to remain in Camden. During his years there, Whitman became a friend of Thomas Eakins, an artist from Philadelphia, Pennsylvania, at a period when these two men of 19th-century American culture admired each other's work. Moreover, each man created something new and American. In fact, Eakins even photographed Whitman and painted his portrait.

Today, the Walt Whitman House serves as the Walt Whitman Cultural Arts Center. The Arts Center is a multi-cultural literary, performing and visual arts center dedicated to continuing the legacy of Walt Whitman, the famous American poet, for artistic purposes. The Center also ensures that Whitman's legacy is accessible to the residents of Camden and to many visitors of the city.

Besides the Walt Whitman House, the history of aviation represents yet another attraction in the Delaware River Area. This aviation-related site is known as the Air Victory Museum. The museum can be found at the South Jersey Regional Airport in Lumberton, New Jersey.

The mission of Air Victory Museum is threefold. First and foremost is education. It educates the youth of our communities about technological advances and encourages them to continue their education and make their own advances. Second, the museum celebrates these advances. And third, it honors the people in aviation that were responsible for these advances.

In addition to the Air Victory Museum, visitors may want to stop by Whitesbog Village, which is the birthplace of the cultivated blueberry in Pemberton, New Jersey. The village offers a tour that is a 5-mile automobile loop around Whitesbog's system of bogs, blueberry fields, reservoirs, canals, and pine forests.

The Driving Tour Guide interprets Whitesbog's natural environment and the impact of the past iron, timber, and agricultural industries on the land. The tour commences in the Whitesbog Village commons located in the grassy area across the road from the water tower. Meanwhile, nature lovers can also experience the Old Bog Nature Trail Guide in Whitesbog Village.

The state of New Jersey is also where visitors can find the Worthington State Forest that runs more than 7 miles along the Kittatinny Ridge in Warren County, on the New Jersey side of the Delaware River, just north of the Delaware Water Gap in the Delaware Water Gap National Recreation Area. The park offers camping, hiking and canoeing on the Delaware River. The forest includes the 1,085-acre Dunnfield Creek Natural Area (258 acres of it is a glacial lake) surrounded by a Chestnut Oak Forest reached by a steep and rocky climb along the Appalachian Trail. Meanwhile, Mount Tammany, at 1,527 feet, offers views of the Delaware Water Gap.

In addition to New Jersey, Pennsylvania offers residents and visitors attractions along the Delaware River. Some of the state's attractions include the Zane Grey Museum, Bristol Riverside Theater, Bowman's Hill Tower, Crossing Vineyards and Winery, David Library of the American Revolution, Buck's County Civil War Museum, Churchville Park and Nature Center, Bowman's Hill Wildflower Preserve, The Bucks County Playhouse, the New Hope and Ivyland Railroad, and William Penn's Riverside Manor.

The Upper Delaware Scenic and Recreational River in Lackawaxen, Pennsylvania is where people can see the Zane Grey Museum. The museum displays both the work of a popular Western author named Zane Grey and an exhibit for John Roebling, a civil engineer who designed the famous Brooklyn Bridge in New York City. The Zane Grey Museum also features information about the Lackawaxen and Delaware Aqueduct (a bridge that runs 535 feet from Minisink Ford, New York to Lackawaxen, Pennsylvania over the Delaware River) that Roebling designed about twenty years before he designed the Brooklyn Bridge.

Zane Grey Museum show cases Grey's different photographs and books in the rooms that served as his office of study. The museum also has information about Roebling who designed and oversaw construction of the Lackawaxen and Delaware Aqueduct, the oldest expansion bridge in America that is still being used today. Zane Grey and John Roebling were main contributors to the history, landscape texture, and cultural development of the Upper Delaware Valley during the 1800s.

Moving on to Bristol, Pennsylvania, the Bristol Riverside Theater was first opened on the corner of Radcliffe and Market Streets in 1987 where it presented live productions and attracted theater artists from around the world to its stage. Today, the theater coordinates nine main stage productions. Many of its programs are geared toward children and to all the performing arts.

Parallel to the Lower Delaware on River Road is where you can see Bowman's Hill Tower standing in Washington Crossing, Pa. This observation tower offers an expansive, scenic view of the Delaware River Region. And as the seasons change, so do the color and visual experiences change at the Tower, making return trips enjoyable for guests and residents each year.

In addition to Bowman's Hill Tower, residents and visitors can see both the Crossing Vineyards and Winery and David Library of the American Revolution in Washington Crossing.

Crossing Vineyards and Winery is located on a 200 year-old estate in Buck County, Pa., less than a mile from the place where George Washington crossed the Delaware River in 1776.

David Library of the American Revolution is a privately owned, nonprofit foundation dedicated to the study of American history circa 1750 to 1800. The mission of the library is to collect and disperse information on the period and support related programs. The David Library is a specialized research institution; it is open to the general public upon completion of an easy registration form and admission to the library is free. Travel to Doylestown, Pa. and that's where you can see the Bucks County Civil War Museum. The museum is home to numerous artifacts related to the Civil War on subjects dealing with Doylestown, the War in general, and the 104th Pa. Volunteer Infantry Regiment. The articles on display are on temporary or permanent loan from area collectors and history buffs. Doylestown also offers people a thriving arts scene.

Moving on to Churchville, Pa. is where you will discover the Churchville Park and Nature Center. The mission of Churchville Nature Center is to instill an application and awareness of nature in all people through education and to inspire responsible environmental stewardship with a commitment to the preservation of natural resources and wildlife.

Another historic Pennsylvania town on the Delaware River, which is quite popular in the area and throughout America offering numerous attractions to visitors, is New Hope.

New Hope is full of tree-lined streets and showcases attractive old buildings attest to the slower pace favored by locals, who enjoy the arts and strolling by the river. And although New Hope feels a lot more rural than big cities, it is only 30 miles from Philadelphia and about 18 miles from Trenton, New Jersey.

Moreover, New Hope is a popular destination with vacationers. The town has many popular restaurants and inns as well as charming stores that sell local produce and crafts. Each October, residents dress up for the annual Halloween special and families enjoy the "Polar Express" at Christmastime.

Yet three key points of interest that come to my mind in New Hope consist of Bowman's Hill Wildflower Preserve, the Bucks County Playhouse, New Hope and Ivyland Railroad, and Bucks County Riverboats.

Bowman's Hill Wildflower Preserve displays an extraordinary array of plants native to Pennsylvania and the Delaware Valley Region. The Preserve focuses strictly on native plants, in distinction from botanical gardens that may include natives in their collections. The property is open from 8:30 a.m. to sunset and the Visitor Center and Twinleaf Shop are open from 9 a.m. to 5 p.m.

Next attraction in New Hope is the Bucks County Playhouse. The Playhouse, which opened in 1939, is the State Theater of Pennsylvania and is a national landmark for Broadway Plays. Some celebrities that performed at Bucks County Playhouse include Merv Griffin, William Shatner, George C. Scott, Liza Minnelli, Loretta Swit, Don Knotts, and John Travolta.

Anyone who is looking for the best in Broadway entertainment at a fraction of the price should visit the Bucks County Playhouse or its sister theaters in the Pocono Playhouse in Mountainhome, Pa. or the Open Air Theater in Washington's Crossing State Park in New Jersey.

The third New Hope attraction that draws train and railroad history buffs is the New Hope and Ivyland Railroad. Once you are onboard a New Hope and Ivyland Railroad train, you will travel through the rolling hills and valleys of Bucks County, Pa. Once on the steam engine train, passengers will experience the sights, sounds, and romance of the Golden Era of Steam Railroading.

The New Hope train ride is something passengers won't forget as they ride on restored 1920s vintage passenger coaches, antique bar car, the steam locomotive or one of the railroad's historic diesel locomotives. Passengers for regular excursion trains may board at the New Hope or Lahaska Station. Passengers may detrain at either station and take a later train back to their originating station. All trains leave the Lahaska Station twenty minutes past the hour and the last train of the day ends in New Hope.

From New Hope, you may want to head to Upper Black Eddy, Pennsylvania, home of the Bucks County Riverboats. Bucks County Riverboat Company operates out of Keller's Landing in

Lower Delaware in the foreground with the Bucks County Playhouse and other buildings in New Hope, Pennsylvania seen in the background.

Photo by Stephen Harris.

Bucks County. The River Otter, a 52-foot coast guard certified boat, is equipped to provide riders with a memorable excursion on the wild and scenic Delaware River. The Riverboat Company's mission is to offer spectacular educational, recreational, and entertainment experiences for groups of all purposes and ages.

Outside of New Hope, another interesting, historic attraction for visitors of Pennsylvania is William Penn's 3-storied, brick Pennsbury Manor House located on land formed by the Lower Delaware River between Morrisville and Bristol, Pennsylvania. Although Penn only lived in Pennsbury Manor for two years (1700-1702), it was his favorite residence.

William Penn was a great leader-minister, speaker and writer of the most extreme seat of the Puritan movement, the Society of Friends (commonly known as Quakers, which were Christians that originated in 17th century England). Penn was also an active member of the newly developing Whig Party that evolved during the 18th century. Furthermore, Penn was a close friend of the Stuart Kings who ruled Britain from 1603 to 1714. He also advised the Stuart Monarchs and even influenced their decisions. Because of his influence, Penn rescued thousands of non-conformists from religious persecution in France, Holland, Ireland, Germany, and England. Yet the governmental entity of Pennsylvania was the zenith of his public career. This was William Penn the gifted administrator with personal power and prominent, well-respected public figure.

But at Pennsbury, Pennsylvania, another side of Penn is revealed. The entire Pennsbury estate: the buildings, landscaping, etc. gives us a deep insight to his personal tastes and habits. The wide doorways, spaciousness of the rooms, and casement windows with their view of the countryside, all show William Penn as the visionary and the imaginative.

Moving onward from historic attractions to trails in Pennsylvania, a popular trail in that state is the Schuylkill River (tributary of the Delaware River) Trail. This trail typically follows the riverbank and is a multi-use trail for bicycling, walking, jogging, and other outdoor activities. Today, the trail runs from Philadelphia, through Manayunk to the village of Mont Clare. Moreover, there is a section of trail beginning at Pottstown and running upriver toward Reading. Plans are underway to finish the trail from the Delaware River to Reading.

In addition to the Delaware River Byway, there's another greenway, specifically the East Coast Greenway, which runs through Pennsylvania. The East Coast Greenway commences in Morrisville (Bucks County), Pa. where travelers cross the Delaware River using the Calhoun Street Bridge from Trenton, New Jersey. This trail runs along the Delaware River as it winds its way through Bucks County, which includes the towns of Tullytown, Falls Township, Bristol Borough, Bristol Township and Bensalem, until it reaches Center City Philadelphia.

In Center City, the East Coast Greenway uses Spring Garden Street to cross the city. Next as it moves through West Philadelphia, then parallels the Schuylkill River until it meets the Delaware River at Fort Mifflin, behind the Philadelphia International Airport. Finally, the trail runs along the Delaware River through Delaware County until it comes to the Delaware State Border.

As for sightseers, the Philadelphia Canoe Club, in the Fairmount Park area, organizes excursions along local rivers and streams, such as the Schuylkill and Delaware rivers. The Canoe Club coordinates trips conducive to sightseeing along with challenging attempts to conquer the area's whitewater rapids.

For those who enjoy canoeing, you can rent a canoe in Wilmington, Delaware, begin paddling down the Delaware River on the Pennsylvania side, and get picked up down the river two hours later in Delaware. The river does most of the work as it leaves you free to enjoy viewing Brandywine Creek State Park in Wilmington where you can see turtles, carp, bass, blue herons, and deer.

Another place of interest people can visit in Pennsylvania is Delaware Canal State Park. This park follows the Delaware River from Easton to Bristol, paralleled by Pennsylvania Routes 611 and 32. This park has an historic canal and 60-mile towpath, many miles of river coastline and eleven river islands. From farm fields to historic towns, guests of Delaware Canal State Park will enjoy the changing scenery along its corridor.

Delaware Canal State Park offers a variety of environmental education programs that include guided walks and hands-on activities where participants can understand, appreciate, and develop a sense of stewardship toward cultural and natural resources.

The sixty-mile-long Delaware Canal towpath extends from Easton to Bristol, Pa. and is a National Recreation Trail. Today, joggers, bicyclists, cross-county skiers and bird watchers use the towpath. In addition, there's a 30-mile stretch of parallel trials with five connecting bridges that allow visitors to choose among eleven different options of loop length and distance. Each loop leads you through wooded in-lands, quaint towns and scenic river views.

Water trail users can see wildlife along a main migratory route for waterfowl and songbirds. Anglers can catch American shad and bass. The canal also contains many warm water game fish. Canoeing is also popular in the canal on the Delaware River. Canoeists can launch their boats from public ramps in Pennsylvania and New Jersey to enjoy the water trail that includes beautiful views of Nockamixon Cliffs and River Islands natural areas.

The Nockamixon Cliffs Natural Area composes sheer north-facing cliffs that tower 300 feet above the river. The shale cliffs are located at the curve in the Delaware, between Kintnersville and Narrowsville (both towns are in Bucks County, Pa.) Visible from both the Delaware River and New Jersey, these cliffs prevail over the landscape of the whole area. In certain places, series of rock shelves and deeply cut ravines containing rivulets and seeps provide habitat for an array of cliff and forest plant communities. The rock looks like to be bare in winter, but is well covered by vegetation in summer.

Due to their north-facing aspect, Nockamixon Cliffs get little direct sunlight. This cool habitat supports an alpine-arctic plant community that is unusual to find this far south. In Pennsylvania, some of these plants are rare or endangered. Directly across the Delaware River in New Jersey, an opposite set of circumstances happens, making habitat for unusually arid plants.

Nockamixon Cliffs originated geologically from reddish mud and sands carried by torrential streams from the northwest. Large amounts of these sediments were deposited into temporary shallow lakes. The resulting shale and red sandstone can still be found throughout the area. They are bright red and break easily into flakes and fragments.

During the Jurassic Period (period from 144 to 206 million years ago when great plant-eating dinosaurs roamed the earth), the region was subjected to continuous erosion. While some other rock like shale and sandstone were worn away, the tough, water-resistant rock remained allowing the Nockamixon Cliffs to emerge above the surrounding landscape.

In addition to Nockamixon Cliffs, another popular natural area in the Upper Delaware is its River Islands. Both wildlife and humans use the undisturbed areas of the Delaware River Islands for recreation and rest. The islands provide a significant corridor for migrating birds. Publicly owned river islands also enhance recreational opportunities for kayakers, canoeists, and fishermen. Moreover, the islands are part of the water trail used by canoeists and other small boaters on the Delaware.

Some river islands, like Hendrick Island, were originally part of the main coastline, but most islands are apart from the river itself. Stone and silt left by glacial waters almost 10,000 years ago is what formed the substrate of these islands. In addition, water, wind or wildlife eventually deposited seeds on the islands. As plants grow on the islands, the roots bind the substrate materials together. Although the islands are stable, the shape, size and location of these islands shift slightly with the movements of the river.

Delaware Canal State Park manages the Delaware River Islands Natural Area, which includes (from north to south) Loors Island, Whippoorwill Island, Old Sow Island, Raubs Island, the Lynn Island Group, and the Hendrick Island Group. With the exception of Hendrick Island, all these river islands are situated close to Raubsville (located in Northampton County, Pa.) and Kintnersville, Pa. The main island at Hendrick is designated as a Special Management Area because of its archaeological significance. All of the islands are delicate environments and support critical habitat for birds, other wildlife, and many rare plants. Because of these delicate environments, no hunting or camping is allowed in the Delaware River Islands Natural Area.

Another park that people can enjoy in Pennsylvania is Neshaminy State Park. Neshaminy is a 339-acre park located along the Delaware River in Lower Bucks County. The park takes its name from Neshaminy Creek that joins the Delaware River at this point. Neshaminy State Park's most popular attractions are its swimming pools and picnic areas. Boating access to the Delaware River is also provided at the marina.

In addition to other attractions that I already mentioned, the state of Pennsylvania is home to the Delaware State Forest. Delaware State Forest covers 80,267 acres in Pike, Monroe, North Hampton and Carbon counties in Pennsylvania. Most of the forest lies in Pike County. Named for the Delaware River, the forest is characteristic of the Pocono Region, with remote glacial lakes and bogs rich with wildlife, plants and scenic beauty.

Regarding recreation, over 740 permanent campsites have been leased on the Delaware State Forest. It also has a major hiking trail that traverses about 30 miles of southern Pike County. The trail highlights mountain streams, swamps, varieties of forest and other natural features found on the Pocono Plateau. In the winter, 90 miles of snowmobile trails are open to the public. This system provides for short or long trail rides. Trail grooming is conducted on about 35 miles of this trail network; snowmobile registration is required.

In addition to what the Delaware State Forest offers to residents and visitors of Pennsylvania, two communities in Pennsylvania and one in New Jersey recently became revitalized and redeveloped along the Delaware River.

As part of its redevelopment and revitalization, the City of Chester, Pennsylvania is reconnecting with its residents to its waterfront on the Delaware River. For this reason, the city acquired 1,400 feet of land to extend the Chester Riverwalk along the Delaware. With the addition of the Chester Riverwalk to the existing facilities on the waterfront, including the new green space and boat ramps, the City of Chester has transformed into one of the best places in the whole Philadelphia area for people to view and interact with the Delaware River.

Meanwhile, Bucks County, Pa. has become a new riverfront community on the Delaware River. Waterside Bensalem Development, a member of the Mignatti family of companies, recently gave Bucks County's waterfront a new look consisting of a mixed-use community. Waterside Bensalem built a unique architectural design (based on Second Empire, Italianate and Colonial styles) that gives Bucks County residents an "old world" feel. The architectural design is composed of balconies, porches and bay windows, all with the objective of enhancing riverfront views. Today, the Bucks County community showcases residential homes of all types, including town homes, condos and single-family homes, incorporated with 53,000 square feet of retail and office space.

Besides riverfront revitalization and redevelopment projects that recently took place in Pennsylvania along the Delaware River, North Camden, New Jersey, located just north of downtown Camden and across the Delaware River from Center City Philadelphia, will gradually become a more attractive waterfront community.

Despite decades of decline, now the community of North Camden is changing as over $600 million in private investment is proposed for downtown Camden over the next eight years. As part of its long-term waterfront park plan, North Camden's Riverfront State Prison will be closing and with that vacant land, the North Camden community will address economic development, housing, infrastructure, public safety, parks and open space over the next decade.

Digressing to recreation on and near the Delaware River in Pennsylvania, New York, and New Jersey, Wilmington, Delaware and other parts of Delaware also offer river recreation with trails that provide walkers, joggers, hikers, and bicyclists clear vantage points of the Delaware River or Bay.

In fact, there are four popular Delaware State Parks that offer people natural, scenic, trails that run along the Delaware River or Bay. These trails travel through a significant statewide greenway that helps preserve the variety of plants, animals, and habitats unique to Delaware.

North of Wilmington is where visitors can find Fox Point State Park, a Delaware state park situated on 171 acres along the Delaware River in New Castle, Del.

The park, which opened in 1995, was built atop a former hazardous waste site that has been rehabilitated under an adaptive reuse program spearheaded by S. Marston Fox and the Fox Point Civic Association. The park is open year round from 8 a.m. until sunset.

Since it's along the Delaware River, Fox Point State Park offers guests many scenic vistas and a view of the working river. The skyline of Philadelphia can be seen to the north and the Delaware Memorial Bridge can be viewed to the south. Fox Point is close to the shipping channel of the Delaware River and container ships, barges, tankers and tugboats pass by regularly.

Furthermore, there are signs on the shore of the river that provide information about the different vessels that can be seen navigating the Delaware River.

In addition to the vistas, park visitors have access to picnic facilities, volleyball courts, horseshoe pits and a playground. Fox Point State Park is also located on the Atlantic Flyway that attracts a variety of migrating birds to the park.

Another park in Delaware to visit is Fort DuPont State Park that is just south of Delaware City off Route 9, hosts 322 acres along the Delaware River. Open year-round, the park provides opportunities for passive recreation including fishing, hiking, and picnicking. Besides passive recreation, a self-guided tour of the park gives joggers and walkers a lot of space to explore its rich history.

For people interested in more active recreation, Fort DuPont State Park offers tennis courts, basketball courts, and a ball field. Named after Rear Admiral Samuel Francis du Pont, the Fort was used as a military base from the Civil War through World War II. After World War II, the Fort was turned over to the state of Delaware.

The third Delaware State Park is Cape Henlopen State Park located near Lewes, Del. Home of the great walking dune and a World War II observation tower, Cape Henlopen is a 3,000-acre park that features sand dunes, a nature center, guided nature trails, fishing, swimming, tennis, and offers travelers ideal spots to take in spectacular views of the Delaware Bay. Visitors can hike the 0.6-mile Seaside Nature Trail or wander onto the 1,800-foot-long Cape Henlopen fishing pier that extends into the Bay.

Finally, residents and visitors can explore Battery Park in Delaware City, Delaware. The park, located along the Delaware River, provides a scenic river front setting for many recreational activities. Within the area people will discover Pea Patch Island, a 90-acre heron-nesting ground for nine different species of birds located in the Delaware River across from Delaware City and the New Jersey shoreline beyond. Both scenes are ideal for photographers. The restored stonewalled lock from the original route of the Chesapeake and Delaware Canal, dated back to 1829, is also in Battery Park.

Besides Battery Park, the Texaco refinery located near Delaware City is one of the main industrial facilities in this area.

The refinery occupies a site consisting of over 900 acres and has a rated crude oil capacity of 140,000 barrels per day. Group tours of the refinery complex can be arranged providing visitors with spectacular insights into an industrial process that is important to their lives.

Indeed, waterside parks in New York, New Jersey, Pennsylvania, and Delaware attract many people to the Delaware River but so do recreational activities such as boating, paddling, fishing, and hiking.

Boaters can now access the Delaware River by going on different boat ramps mostly located in New Jersey and Pennsylvania. In New Jersey, some ramps boaters can access include the Belvidere New Jersey Ramp (it's on Front St. in Belvidere, NJ fifty yards south of the Delaware River Bridge), Bordentown, NJ Municipal Boat Ramp, Bulls Island State Park, NJ (on Route 29 near Stockton, NJ), Burlington Marina (located in Burlington City, NJ just off of Route 130 and High St., near the Burlington-Bristol Bridge), Byram, NJ (off Route 29 three miles north of Stockton, NJ), and Florence, NJ (located on Delaware Ave. off of Route 130).

Other New Jersey boat ramps include the Gloucester City Marina, Lambertville Boat Ramp, Pennsauken Boat Ramp, Poxono Ramp (located six miles north of the I-80 bridge on the NJ side of the river), and the Trenton, NJ Ramp (a public ramp that provides access to the lower, tidal section of the river).

In Pennsylvania, boaters can access ramps that include Martins Creek, Pa, Matamoras, Pa. (on 549 one and a half miles north of the Port Jervis, New York bridge), Milford Beach Ramp (on Route 209 in Milford, Pa. ¼ mile north of Route 206 bridge), Morrows Marina in Ridley Park, Pa., New Hope Boat Ramp, and Philadelphia - Linden Ave. (public ramp in NE Philadelphia).

More ramps in Pennsylvania consist of Scott's Park (located at the confluence of the Lehigh and Delaware rivers on the Pa. side in downtown Easton), Smithfield Beach (boat launch that's within the Delaware Water Gap National Recreation Area; it's in the center of Pennsylvania's Pocono Mountains), and Yardley, Pa. (ramp located about ¼ mile south of I-95; it's hard to use in the summer because of shallow water there).

Besides New Jersey and Pennsylvania boat ramps, boaters can access a ramp in Narrowsburg, New York (on Route 97),

Lewes Boat Ramp in Lewes, Del., and one in Woodland Beach (in Woodland Beach, Delaware).

In addition to accessing boat ramps in neighboring states along the Delaware River, boaters and paddlers can enjoy an exciting time on the Lower Tidal Delaware River in Pennsylvania. However, they must be aware of their surroundings to have a safe experience.

They must know that the Tidal Delaware River is an active river that passes under historic bridges, through lively urban centers, and serves as a main thoroughfare for very big ships. Both paddlers and boaters need to stay safe on the river and be alert for huge, fast ships especially those navigating in the shipping lane and anchorage. Other ships and tugs that accompany these fast ships also make very large wakes.

Kayakers and boaters on the tidal Delaware should also be experienced. Open canoes without floatation devices are not recommended. Furthermore, you should not boat alone, be certain that you are visible to other boaters, and be aware of your surroundings. You must also watch out for floating debris especially after heavy rain. a boater needs to be aware that much of the river is urbanized with industry and ports so river walls and piers may present obstacles. You must be prepared for inclement weather such as rain, wind, and cold too. Finally, stay clear of security risk areas and communicate with the Coast Guard, marine police, and other security personnel.

In regards to safety tips on paddling and boating, wearing your life jacket is critical when you are on the Delaware. About 80 % of all recreational boating fatalities occur to people who don't wear a life jacket. Even the best paddlers sometimes capsize or swamp their boats so bring extra clothing in a waterproof bag and be ready to swim. If the water appears too dangerous to swim in, don't go boating. If you capsize, cling onto your boat, unless it presents a life-threatening situation. If you are floating in a current, position yourself on the upriver side of the capsized boat. In addition, a boater should scout ahead whenever possible; get to know the river, and avoid surprises by getting a forecast before he goes. Sudden rain and winds can turn a nice trip into a risky, unpleasant venture.

More paddler safety rules include: wear wading or tennis shoes with wool socks when on the boat; never take your boat over a low-head dam; take your boat around any waterway section in which you feel uncertain; and never boat alone (boating safety is enhanced with numbers). Moreover, never tie a rope to yourself or to another boater, especially a child. More safety tips consist of filing a float plan indicating where you are going and when you will return. And if you collide with an obstruction in a kayak, lean toward it. This will normally prevent flooding or capsizing the boat.

The Tidal Delaware River presents a number of safety challenges for sail, paddling, and motor craft. Very large commercial boats traverse the shipping lane that runs the length of the tidal river (lane is marked by red and green buoys). These ships can be fast moving and can't stop or slow down easily. In addition to avoiding ships, recreational boaters need to be on the alert for huge wakes generated by ships. Kayakers can paddle the main stem Tidal Delaware, however a high level of expertise is needed to negotiate wakes, including those chummed up by maneuvering tugboats. In addition to large ships and wakes, boaters must contend with river hazards like currents and tides, boat traffic (both small and large), floating debris, piers, river walls, and bridge abutments.

The tidal surge up the Delaware River is so powerful that the river changes direction four times daily. Boaters, specifically those in manpowered craft, must consider the changing tides. A thorough review of daily tide change forecasts should be made for the specific portion of the river that you plan to traverse. Paddlers should paddle with the tide in one direction and then paddle back to the starting point after the tidal current has switched direction. A large degree of planning, caution, and experience is needed to be certain that the tidal current is traveling with you from start to finish. Before a paddler or boater gets on the river, he must make sure he has clearly identified rest stops and emergency bail out locations along the way.

Where not to anchor is another important rule of thumb for a boater or paddler. Anyone floating or riding on the Delaware must not anchor in the shipping lane, at designated anchorages or under bridges. Other places to avoid include active industrial, port, and pipeline facilities. It is recommended that you maintain a 25 to 50 foot distance from these areas and do not tie into private piers. An area of heavy ship traffic, anchorages, terminals, and piers happens between the Walt Whitman and Ben Franklin bridges. The shipping lane is not marked along this stretch so remain aware, alert, and keep to the shallowest water whenever you are moving through this area. In addition, look out for tour boat and ferry activity near Penn's Landing and Bristol, Pennsylvania. Finally, remain clear of utilities and other structures such as the pipeline upriver of the Burlington Bristol Bridge on the New Jersey side.

Besides boating, there are many fishing opportunities in the Delaware River. Now that the Delaware River is cleaner, there are male striped bass up to 20 pounds feeding on brown and rainbow trout all summer in the upper reaches of the Delaware between Pennsylvania, New Jersey and New York.

But to take advantage of the fish swimming in the river, fishermen must be aware of all the rules before they go fishing. On the Delaware between New York and Pennsylvania, a valid New York or Pennsylvania fishing license is required for all anglers (age 16 and older) when fishing from a boat or from either bank. Moreover, New Jersey licenses are not valid on the river between New York and Pennsylvania.

Anyone fishing on the Delaware between Pennsylvania and New York must obtain a summary book of regulations and laws with his or her license. Then an angler should refer to the boundary/border waters section of that book and follow the regulations for creel limit, size, and open season. A fisherman may use a maximum of two lines and trout stamps are required with a Penn. license to take, kill, or possess any trout. In addition, fishing licenses may be bought from local sporting goods stores or other state license-issuing agents.

Regarding licensed Pennsylvania anglers, new striped bass regulations took affect in April 2009. Today, licensed Pennsylvania anglers fishing the Delaware River can now harvest striped bass and hybrid striped bass from April 1 to May 31, a season which has been closed by the Pennsylvania Fish and Boat Commission since 1992.

Under these new regulations, fishermen can harvest two striped bass per day between 20 to 26 inches during the 2-month season. These Pennsylvania fishing regulations allow some harvest of male striped bass, while still protecting most of the spawning female striped bass. For the rest of the year, there is a 28-inch minimum length and a two fish per day creel limit.

Fishing and boat officials in both Pennsylvania and New York also urge licensed anglers on the Delaware River to be responsible. Responsible angling consists of following fishing rules: handling fish carefully to avoid injury; keep only the fish you plan to use; never stock fish or plants in public waters; pay attention to safe angling and safer boating regulations; remove all mud and drain all water from boats before leaving access site; and don't disturb nesting birds.

More rules include: do not release live bait into the water, dispose of water from a bait bucket on land, don't transport fish or aquatic plants from one body of water to another, don't dispose of fish carcasses or byproducts in the river, properly dispose of used fishing line, and leave the area as clean as you found it.

Like what New York and Pennsylvania requires for someone to obtain a Delaware River fishing license, anyone 16 and older needs to have a valid license to fish New Jersey fresh waters with hand line, rod and line, or longbow and arrow. However, no fishing license is needed for anglers under 16.

New Jersey also requires that fishing licenses be worn in a conspicuous place on one's outer clothing while engaged in fishing, and must be displayed to law enforcement personnel on request. Another important fishing rule pertaining to anglers, which are New Jersey residents between the ages of 16 to 69, states that it's unlawful for any person to get a resident license unless they have lived in New Jersey for six months immediately prior to the time of application. And regarding trout fishing, no one between 16 and 69 shall take, attempt to take, or kill trout without a valid fishing license that has a trout stamp attached to it.

Once anglers meet the state of New Jersey's fishing requirements, they will find many fishing opportunities for warm water and cold water fish in that specific portion of the Delaware. Over the past ten years, fishermen have caught many striped bass and American shad there during the spring. They also have many opportunities to catch northern pike, muskies, and walleye in the New Jersey stretch of the Delaware River.

Along with New Jersey, the state of Delaware offers anglers ideal fishing spots. For example, Wilmington, Del., is a good location for those that wish to engage in some fly-fishing. Anglers can also fish on the Delaware River shoreline in Delaware where they will find many opportunities to catch sunfish, trout, carp, and bass.

Of course just like in New York, Pennsylvania, and New Jersey, Delaware requires people to obtain a fishing license to fish in tidal and non-tidal waters (like the Delaware River that's mostly non-tidal) within the state. A Delaware fishing license may be obtained from its Dover office or from more than 100 license agents (mostly hardware and sporting goods stores) across the state.

Each fishing license holder must display the license on an outer garment while fishing. Any Delaware resident, who is 16 or older but under 65, is required to have a license to fish in non-tidal waters. In addition, possession of a trout stamp may be required for freshwater trout fishing.

Good fishing spots along the Delaware River can be found in New Jersey, Pennsylvania, and New York. In New Jersey, some of these spots include Bordentown (during the summer and fall, fishing is great for stripers and catfish), Camden (good place to catch carp, catfish, largemouth bass and striped bass).

Today, fishing in the Delaware River is relatively good. Anglers could catch a variety of fish depending upon what portion of the river they are fishing from. It is also interesting to note the history and development of Delaware River fishing.

From the 1870s to the mid-1900s, the Delaware River was known for its spectacular small-mouth bass fishing. In addition, there are many different stories about just how the Delaware River's rainbow trout population started. Yet despite any of these tales, during the 1880s, rainbows were stocked into small feeder streams on the Delaware in Pennsylvania and New York, where they thrived for over 80 years.

The Delaware wasn't known for its trout fishing until the 1960s. The construction of two dams (the Pepacton Dam built on the river's East Branch) in 1961 and (the Cannonsville Reservoir erected on the West Branch) in 1967, changed the upper main part of the river, making the East and West branches into cold-water fisheries, suitable for trout fishing.

The Delaware River contains a large number of brown and rainbow trout. The farther you travel down river, the fewer brown trout you will find. However, the biggest reward in fishing the main stem of the Delaware is the chance to catch huge, wild trout.

Anglers won't catch a lot of fish in the main stem, but the quality of fish there is superb. Most fish in the river's primary stem average from 15 to 18 inches long and weigh between one and two pounds. It is also common to catch fish there that are over 20 inches long.

In addition to the Delaware's trout fishing, it also has a good warm-water fishery. Beneath the cold-water zone, the river still has great bass fishing. During most months of the year, numerous large and small-mouth bass can be reeled in. As fishermen approach the lower section of the river, they can catch striped bass. Striped bass are also caught in the cold-water zone as far up river as Hancock, New York that is over 220 miles from sea. Besides trout and bass, each spring, anglers can catch shad as these fish make their annual run up the river to spawn.

Besides fishing, people can swim in some portions of the Delaware. During the summer, swimming is relatively safe on the New Jersey side of the Delaware Water Gap National Recreation Area and Worthington State Forest. At the east end of the Delaware Water Gap Information Center you'll find a water play/swimming place. People swimming there will certainly have fun but must be aware that the Delaware River frequently has strong, rapid currents so swimmers need to check the currents each time before they go into the river.

The Worthington State Forest Area also has a swimming place in the Delaware River. The south end has rocky ledges for jumping and the north end of this swimming area has a gradual slope. Water there is clear and clean with a very gentle current most of the summer.

However, anyone wanted to participate in water activities must know that the Delaware River contains huge hidden rocks, deep holes, swift currents and underwater ledges. Therefore, it can be very dangerous to swimmers, divers, and anglers. You should never dive into the river or swim in unprotected waters. Fishermen always should wear a safety belt when wading, and fish from the shore when alone.

In addition to boating, fishing, and swimming, you can find some popular places to go tubing and rafting, and camping on the Delaware in New Jersey, Pennsylvania, and New York. In New Jersey, one spot to tube at is in central Jersey (Frenchtown). That is where you can enjoy a four-hour tubing or rafting adventure on the

Delaware River. You can also explore the small islands and sunbathe. In addition, will find little nooks to stop in and swim at your leisure.

Another spot is in Phillipsburg, New Jersey where the Lazy River Outpost is located. This is the spot where your family can enjoy nature and tubing in a natural environment. The Outpost offers adults and children a fun, safe setting where they can engage in river tubing, rafting, kayaking and canoeing in a quiet part of the Middle Delaware.

In Delaware, New Jersey, you'll find the Delaware River Family Campground where families can go tubing and camping in one weekend. Single tubes are available to rent to go tubing on the Delaware and four or eight mile tubing trips are available. The Delaware River Family Campground is also an ideal place to go tubing in the Delaware River Water Gap Area.

Another good place to go tubing on the river is in Point Pleasant (Bucks County) Pennsylvania, just across the river from Stockton, New Jersey. Very mild waters there are ideal for family trips on the Delaware River. Tubing trips and rafting trips are available (rafts hold up to five people) and Bucks County River Country offers snuggle tubes that hold two people.

Tubing in the Poconos, Pa. is also fun for individuals and families. That's where you have a choice of two different tubing trips offered daily (you can meet at the River Beach Campgrounds in Pennsylvania or Kittatinny Campgrounds in New York). Whichever trip you choose, Kittatinny will bring you upriver to a launch site that will give you a three-mile float trip that typically lasts about three hours. You can also rent tubes and rafts in Minisink, Pa. while experiencing the majestic Delaware River in Pennsylvania with Chamberlain Canoes. From the water you will see the natural beauty of the region, smell the fresh air full of the aroma of flowers and plants, and see many birds and other wildlife. Chamberlain Canoes also offers guests Overnight River Camping. Moreover, you can visit Point Pleasant, Penn. that is located near New Hope, Pa. and Point Pleasant is where you can take your children Delaware River tubing across the river from New Jersey.

Like New Jersey and Pennsylvania, Delaware River Tubing is also popular in New York. For example, in Barryville, New York, Indian Head Canoes River rafting is offered to those that are interested. Indian Head also offers visitors an array of overnight lodging, deluxe cabins, riverside log cabins, and campgrounds.

Located in Barryville and Matamoras, Pennsylvania, Indian Head Canoes River rafting is nestled between the wild forest mountains of the Poconos and Catskills.

Finally, you can participate in water activities at dirondack Adventures in North Creek, New York. River tubing is available there from the third weekend in June to Labor Day. Adirondack Adventures also supplies guests with all the equipment and food (except sleeping bags) for two days of rafting and one night of camping. In addition, you can arrange multi-day trips by raft, canoe, etc. and a night of camping.

Chapter 5
Some Historical highlights of the Delaware River itself, Its towns, navigational system, region, geology, terrain and ecology

In the middle of the 20th-century, shipbuilding flourished along the Delaware River. Since 1933, cargo ships of all sizes, tankers, container-carrying vessels, barges accompanied by tugboats, and many recreational boats create a steady flow of traffic in the port of Philadelphia, Penn. The oil refinery business also boomed along the Delaware River during the 20th-century as hundreds of tankers regularly transported oil back and forth to and from the Lower Delaware.

During the early 1920s, bathing and swimming in the Delaware River was a popular activity. In the late 18th and early 19th centuries, a handful of Dutch settlers and a group of people known as the Connecticut Yankees were the primary arrivals to the Delaware River Area. The Irish, who helped build the Delaware and Hudson Canal, followed them. The Germans, who came to farm the land, followed the Irish. Overall, the Delaware River was a lifeline for Pennsylvania and New Jersey colonists who relied on the waterway as their only supply route.

In addition to those who started to settle along the Delaware, during the 1800s, a number of new waterway developments took place on the Delaware River. In Philadelphia, the city had canal projects in progress to reach the interior land. In 1825, the Schuylkill Canal was built, extending from Fairmont to Port Carbon above Reading, Pennsylvania, a length of 108 miles. Thanks to the canal, supplies and coal were then transported to and from Philadelphia. A second canal, the Lehigh Coal Canal, began operating in 1827 and had downstream navigation for 56 miles. In 1828, a third canal, the Delaware and Hudson Canal (D and H Canal), was built and opened to navigation.

The D and H Canal began at Rondout Creek, New York between Kingston (where the creek fed into the Hudson River) and Rosendale, New York. From there it continued southwest alongside Rondout Creek to Ellenville, continuing through the valley of the Basher Kill and Neversink River to Port Jervis on the

Delaware River. From there the canal ran northwest on the New York side of the Delaware River, crossing into Pennsylvania at Lackawaxen and flowing on the north bank of the Lackawaxen River to Honesdale, Pa.

Yet another canal, the Chesapeake Bay and Delaware Canal (C and D Canal), opened for business in 1829. From 1829 to 1919 with the erection of the C and D Canal, a 14-mile-long, 10-foot-deep, 66-foot-wide navigation channel at the waterline, which was 36 feet wide along the channel bottom, connected the Chesapeake Bay and Delaware River.

During that 90-year period, teams of horses and mules towed freight and passenger barges, schooners and sloops through the C and D Canal. Cargoes consisted of almost every useful item of daily life: grain, lumber, farm products, cotton, fish, coal, iron and whiskey. Packet lines were eventually established to move freight through the waterway. One line, the Ericsson Line, operated between Baltimore, Maryland and Philadelphia, Pennsylvania, and continued to carry passengers and freight through the canal until the 1940s.

Between 1935 and 1938, the C and D Canal was improved as it was deepened to 27 feet and widened to 250 feet to accommodate more cargo and bigger ships. Prior to that improvement, the Philadelphia District took over the operation of the canal in 1933. The "new" C and D Canal opened in 1927.

In 1919, the canal was purchased by the federal government for $2.5 million and was designated the "Intra-coastal Waterway Delaware River to Chesapeake Bay, Delaware and Maryland." Cargo tonnage peaked in 1872 with over 1.3 million tons transiting the C and D Canal.

Finally, there's the Delaware Canal that was built in 1832. From 1832 to 1931, canal boats plied the Delaware Canal, hauling coal from the mines of Mauch Chuck, Pennsylvania to Bristol, Pennsylvania where the tidewaters of the Delaware Bay made the Delaware River deep enough to be navigable year round. How the Delaware Canal became a reality is linked to the Delaware and Lehigh rivers in Pennsylvania. Without the rivers nearby to act as water sources, the canal would never have been a possibility.

But while having rivers close by was needed for the canal, it was also a curse. During the canal's heyday, river floods caused long-term damages and often stopped canal traffic for months at a time. Yet now is no different as floods can damage the Delaware Canal towpath and canal structures.

When it was originally completed, the Delaware Canal connected with the Lehigh Navigation System at Easton, Pa. and helped to develop the anthracite coal industry in Pennsylvania's Upper Lehigh Valley. Today, the 60-mile Delaware Canal is the only remaining continuously intact canal of the great towpath canal building era of the early and mid-19th century.

In the 19th century, the area's canals were popular. Canals provided a convenient and economical means of transporting natural resources such as coal to urban areas such as Philadelphia and New York. Meanwhile, Philadelphia focused on shipbuilding that became a very significant industry for the city. In 1837, the *U.S.S. Pennsylvania*, launched in Philadelphia, was the biggest ship in the world. Speaking of ships, by the mid-19th century, oar-powered "tugging" boats were replaced by bigger and stronger-hulled craft powered by steam engines. These mechanized tugboats have been a critical part of the daily life and commerce of rivers like the Delaware ever since.

Meanwhile during the early 19th century, steamboats replaced schooners and sloops as the main mode of transportation for persons traveling on their summer vacations from Philadelphia, Pennsylvania, Baltimore, Maryland and Wilmington, Delaware to Cape May, New Jersey. Also in the 1800s the state of Delaware experienced significant developments on the Delaware River. During that period, all water routes such as the Delaware River saw more use due to cost and accessibility. Shipping and shipbuilding also continued to be very important to the city's commerce because most steamboats on the Delaware were made at Wilmington. Steamboat lines ferrying passengers up and down the Delaware River and Bay also began in the 19th-century. In fact, the first oceangoing trip of a paddle steamer named "Albany" occurred in 1808 when the vessel steamed from the Hudson River along the coast to the Delaware River. This steamer was strictly used for the purpose of moving a riverboat to a new market, but the use of paddle-steamers for coastal trips began soon after that.

Besides boats, bridges symbolized an important water transportation link during the 19th century. For example, in order to cross the Christina River (a Delaware River tributary), one of the first bridges was built in the 1800s to replace the ferry that crossed the Christina River between Wilmington and New Castle, Delaware. This bridge provided new trading opportunities and boosted land values on both sides of the Delaware River. Meanwhile, the Brandywine River (another Delaware River tributary) moves from the plateau, which provided a huge resource for industry. Finally, the Port of Wilmington on the Delaware has been a spectacular harbor for numerous ocean vessels and their cargoes.

Important industries in Delaware also blossomed in the nineteenth century and were mostly based in Wilmington. These industries included flour and textile mills, carriage factories, shipyards, morocco leather plants, and iron foundries. Specifically, shipbuilding was a critical force in the economy during this period as shipyards made schooners, wooden sloops, and fishing boats located in all the port towns along the Delaware River and its tributaries.

Beginning in the late 1800s, more railroads began replacing boats to transport commerce along the Delaware River because trains could carry much more goods at a much faster speed than ships. In 1891, the Pennsylvania Railroad (PRR) was the country's largest coal-hauling railroad, frequently carrying over 100 million tons a year. In addition, it consumed 15 million tons annually just to feed its steam locomotives. Both the PRR and the Reading Railroad in Pennsylvania constructed docks on the Delaware River at Philadelphia to export coal, and to transport imported iron ore from around the world to steel mills in Pittsburgh and Bethlehem, Penn. Railroads began to compete against water carriers on the Delaware in the 1830s and were a huge influence on manufacturing and urban development.

The railroads also carried cement and slate from the Allentown-Bethlehem-Easton Penn. Area. In the 1800s, logging railroads pulled freshly cut timber from small lumber companies throughout the state, transporting to sawmills and rivers. Speaking of timber, during the mid-1800s, over 50 million board feet of hemlock and pine were shipped down river annually. In addition to timber, tanneries were main industries in the Delaware Valley from the 1850s until the 1880s.

Economic development continued during the 19th century and in 1802, Frenchman Eleuthere Irenee du Pont founded a gunpowder mill on the Delaware River near Wilmington,

Delaware. The Du Pont Company soon established Wilmington as the "Chemical Capital of the World."

Ferries were the primary means of crossing the Delaware River until 1804-06, when the first bridge was built on the site of what is now the Trenton Makes Bridge. Railroads were also popular during the early 1800s. John Stevens, a businessman, launched his first steam ferry in 1809. Stevens operated his ferry on the Delaware River between Philadelphia and Trenton, New Jersey. Despite the ferryboats' popularity in the 1800s, ferries have been around on the Delaware River since 1688 when service was first launched between Camden, New Jersey and Philadelphia, Pennsylvania.

Today, ferries remain a primary means of crossing the Delaware River. In fact, now the RiverLink Ferry provides daily transportation between the Camden, New Jersey and Philadelphia, Pennsylvania Waterfronts. RiverLink takes passengers to a variety of attractions that are found on both sides of the river.

Besides ferries, tugboats symbolized the history of Delaware River boats that were working watercraft. By the mid-19th century, oar-powered "tugging" boats were replaced by bigger and tougher-hulled craft powered by steam engines. Such mechanized tugboats have been an important part of the daily life and commerce of the Delaware River ever since.

From the 1800s to the mid-20th century, tugboats hung their sides with lengths of wood as fenders. However, in recent history, the story of Delaware River tugs ended sadly. During the 1980s, the collapse of most of the Delaware River's heavy industrial base brought traumatic changes that altered the workboat business. The Delaware River business was drying up. Gone were the general cargo ships making weekly calls, replaced with huge container ships that called every four to six weeks. It became the end of the way tugboat life had been on the Delaware River for a very long time.

In the early 1700s, shipbuilding industries grew in Philadelphia and Wilmington. In 1750, the Durham boat was a huge wooden boat made by the Durham Boat Company of Durham, Pennsylvania. They were designed by company owner Robert Durham to navigate the Delaware River and transport products to Philadelphia, Pennsylvania and Trenton, New Jersey. Yet the Durham boats are most famous for their use in

RiverLink Ferry and Ben Franklin Bridge with Philadelphia, Pennsylvania in the background.

Photo taken by Jean-Marc Dubus.

Washington's crossing of the Delaware during the American Revolution.

The 18th-century was the era when steamboats were first introduced on rivers like the Delaware and Hudson. One of the early inventors of steamboats was John Fitch. Fitch invented the first paddle steamboat in America in 1786 and it first operated in 1787. In 1790, Fitch operated three steamships, which moved at about three miles an hour on the Delaware River that included one, which provided regular passenger service to Burlington, New Jersey. After the 18th-century ended, the 19th-century became the prime period for steamship navigation on the Delaware River. Hence in 1809, a steamboat named the Phoenix (built at Hoboken, New Jersey) made regular trips to Bordentown, New Jersey where New York City passengers were brought by stagecoach from Bordentown to Washington, New Jersey and thence to New York by boat. The summer of 1812 marked the next steamship to navigate the Delaware; this riverboat was called the "New Jersey." The New Jersey made daily passenger trips to Whitehill, New Jersey, which was the landing beneath Bordentown.

By June 1813, another riverboat named "The Eagle," built in Kensington, New Jersey, began taking regular passenger trips to Burlington, New Jersey. In fact, soon after The Eagle navigated the Delaware, the steamship business increased in New Jersey. Meanwhile, passengers from Camden, New Jersey crossed the river by ferryboats to reach the steamers because back then no steamboat lines had been established in Camden.

Seven years later starting in the 1820s, steamboats running both on the Delaware and Hudson Rivers became part of a through route between New York City, New York and Philadelphia, Pennsylvania. Steamboats also transported passengers from New York City to South Amboy, New Jersey, where they rode on stagecoaches for a trip to Bordentown, New Jersey. From Bordentown, passengers then transferred to a riverboat for the trip to Philadelphia. Then by the 1830s, there was a great demand for steamboat travel on the Delaware River.

In addition to steamboat travel, General George Washington made the river's history even richer in the late 1700s. Washington's crossing of the Delaware, in which he and his crew were steering a Durham boat, occurred on December 25(Christmas Day), 1776 during the American Revolutionary War.

That crossing was the first move in a planned surprise attack organized by Washington against the Hessian forces in Trenton, New Jersey. George Washington led Continental Army troops from Pennsylvania across the icy Delaware River in a challenging and potentially dangerous operation in order to occupy Trenton. Other planned crossings in support of the operation were called off or not successful, but Washington successfully surprised and defeated the troops of Johann Rail quartered in Trenton. Besides the Washington crossing, in the 1760s, timber rafting began developing into a crucial point of the local Delaware River economy.

During the early 1700s, the lumber industry brought thousands of people in Delaware to work in sawmills constructed along the Delaware River. Yet another town on the Delaware that played an important role in the river's history is Trenton, New Jersey. In the early 1700s, Trenton was the head of navigation on the Delaware and became a port for shipping products and grain traveling between Philadelphia and New York City. Trenton was also a main stopping point on the stagecoach line joining the two larger cities. Then in 1727, a chartered ferry connected Trenton with Philadelphia, Pennsylvania, finishing the transportation circle.

Earlier in the Delaware River's history, the first Colonial Settlement occurred in 1681 as William Penn (a Quaker) obtained the title to Pennsylvania in a land grant from King Charles II of England. Penn assigned a commission to select a site with sufficient water frontage on the Delaware River. Penn's agents also arrived on the Delaware River during 1681. In 1682, Penn established the city, Philadelphia, and planned a rectangular grid pattern on 1,200 acres between the Delaware and Schuylkill rivers.

In the mid-1600s, Agustine Herman, a Dutch minister and mapmaker, observed that only a narrow strip of land separated two bodies of water, the Delaware River and Chesapeake Bay. Herman proposed that a waterway be built to join the two. However, this waterway, which later became the Chesapeake Bay and Delaware Canal, wasn't constructed until the late 1820s.

Today, it's known as the Delaware River but in the 1600s, to the Dutch, the Delaware River was the South River, since it was the main waterway through the southern part of New Netherlands (by the same token, they called the Hudson River the North River). The South River Region of New Netherlands has made special and significant contributions to American history. Although early Virginia and New England remained predominately English enclaves, the Delaware Valley was one of the few centers of multiculturalism in the early American colonies, a blend of Dutch, Swedes, English, Germans, Finns, and other settlers. In fact, the Finns brought their distinctive cultural features with them that became an American icon: the log cabin.

During the mid-1600s, many treaties were signed with the Indian tribes for the purchase of their lands. As I just mentioned, Dutch, Swedes, Finns and English settled in the Delaware Valley in the seventeenth-century between 1643 and 1681. The majority of them lived in cabins on prime agricultural land near the Delaware River. Tobacco and fur were their primary commodities for trading. In 1664, the English seized Dutch territory on the Delaware River within the state of Delaware. In 1638, the Swedes started to plant farms along the Delaware River; they lived in peace with the Susquehanna and Lenni-Lennape ("original people") Indians, with whom they traded for furs.

Many decades before Quaker William Penn arrived at the Delaware River Region in the late 1600s, Cornelius Mey, a Dutch explorer, captain, and fur trader, explored the Delaware River and claimed it for Holland in 1623. However, more than ten years prior to Mey's arrival on the Delaware, Henry Hudson, an English explorer and navigator, first mapped the Delaware River (known as South River in the New Netherland colony that followed) in 1609, the same year he discovered the Hudson River (the river farther north), that bears his name. In 1609, Hudson entered the Delaware River and Delaware Bay in search of a trade route to the Far East for a Dutch company.

Yet the name given to the river and the bay didn't become a reality until a year after Hudson's discovery. As I mentioned earlier, when the first settlers arrived in the New World, they met the Lennape Indians. The Europeans changed the Lennape name to Delaware, because the Indians lived on the Delaware River. The river, bay, and later the state, was named after Lord De La Warr, then governor of the Jamestown Colony in Virginia, who probably never saw the Delaware River. Also during 1609, Dutch and Swedish colonists (explorers, traders, and farmers along the Delaware River) established the original European Settlement in the Delaware River Region, which today would be within the state of Pennsylvania. Then in 1615, a navigator from the Netherlands viewed the land site that later became Philadelphia.

During the 17th-century, European settlers transformed the Delaware River Valley landscape by chopping down forests for agriculture, constructing mills to process grains, and to make textiles and paper. Around these mills sprang up towns like Milford, Stockton, and Lambertville in New Jersey, and Easton, Riegelsville, and New Hope in Pennsylvania.

However, Henry Hudson wasn't the earliest explorer of the Delaware River coastline. In fact, the Portuguese and Spanish are believed to have made explorations of the Delaware coast as early as 1526. Prior to the Portuguese and Spanish discovering the coast of Delaware, Giovanni Verrazano became the first European to see the Delaware River while in the Delaware Bay in 1524.

Prior to 1526 and before any Europeans arrived on the banks of the Delaware; the earliest inhabitants on the Delaware River coastline were the American Indians. During the 1500s, the Lenni-Lenape Indians, English settlers later called them the "Delaware" and other tribes first occupied the region and lived mainly by fishing and hunting as they resided in villages along the creeks and rivers (including the Delaware). Village populations ranged from 100 to 300 people, and these villages were relocated often to support population growth. Lenni-Lenape Indians settled along the Delaware River as early as 1400. About 1,000 years ago, early inhabitants of the region knew the Delaware River as Lenapewi Sippu or "river of human beings." And according to historians, the ancestors of Lenni Lenape, likely came from Asia, via the Bering Strait, approximately 10,000 years ago.

As for the history of the Upper Delaware Valley, the Woodland Indians were the first group of people to practice agriculture there dating back to about 1,000 B.C. Then the Woodland Indians stepped aside to the Minsi Indians that first encountered Dutch traders as early as approximately 1614 A.D.

Reiterating history within the Upper Delaware Region, Barryville, New York is one town that depicts the history of the Delaware River. Barryville is named for William T. Barry, postmaster general under President Andrew Jackson. The town grew up around the Delaware and Hudson (D and H) Canal, which opened in 1828 and operated until 1898. The canal ran through what is today the center of the village.

The Upper Delaware River also served as the conduit for timber cut in the Barryville area that was rafted to Philadelphia, Pennsylvania for use in the ship building industry until the mid-19th century.

In addition to Barryville, Port Jervis, New York is an historic town located in the twin valleys of the Delaware and Neversink (tributary of the Delaware) rivers. Port Jervis became a city in 1907 and has long been a transportation center.

From 1875 until 1940, Port Jervis was a significant regional industrial and economic center and shipping depot for bluestone. Citizens who wanted to honor the chief engineer of the D and H Canal, John B. Jervis, who then was overseeing its construction, named the village Port Jervis in 1827. During the 1690s, European settlers first came to the area and the fertile valley had many farms. Port Jervis later was utilized as a boat basin and repair point along the Delaware and Hudson Canal.

Like Barryville and Port Jervis, Narrowsburg, New York is an old Upper Delaware community. In 1853, Narrowsburg was established and the history of the area is tied to the Upper Delaware River, commerce and transportation.

From the late 1700s until the mid-1800s, the town of Narrowsburg was known as the Big Eddy for the huge quiet pool in the river at this location. The town became a favorite stopping place for lumbermen who steered the great timber rafts down the river to the big markets of Trenton, New Jersey and Philadelphia and Easton, Pa.

Moving south to the Lower Delaware Region, Trenton, New Jersey, which is now the capital of New Jersey, is truly a river town that represents part of the Delaware's history. In the early 1900s, most of the Trenton Ferry Historic District was occupied by the Trenton Municipal Wharf that consisted of a warehouse/ terminal building, bulkhead, turning basin, and a wharf. During the early 1930s, river commerce shifted downriver to the location of Trenton's Marine Terminal where Philadelphia and Trenton were main destinations of steamboats. River traffic from Trenton also linked to several other towns along the lower reaches of the Delaware and in 1932, the Delaware River Channel was dredged to twenty feet, making Trenton a port for ocean-going vessels. However, the Philadelphia and New England ports today have since eclipsed the Trenton's significance as a port.

The old Trenton Municipal Wharf Building with a sign on it of Port Trenton (located further downriver on the Delaware).

Photo taken in 1932 by R. C. Maxwell Co. and an advertising sign company in Trenton, New Jersey. Courtesy of Rubenstein Library, Duke University, in Durham, N.C.

South of Port Trenton on the Delaware is another historic port, the Port of Camden in Camden, New Jersey. In 1828, this port was incorporated as a city and for decades just like its neighbor, the Port of Philadelphia, Pa., it was a major, positive, contributor to the overall local and national economy. And during its peak operations that occurred during the early 1900s, the Port of Camden was home to many major businesses that include: RCA Victor (maker of records and phonographs), the New York Shipbuilding Corporation, and Campbell's Soup Company. Today, the South Jersey Port Corporation is the Port Authority for the Port of Camden. The port now handles domestic and international bulk as well as break bulk cargoes at its two terminals.

In the late 1700s, General George Washington and his soldiers occupied Trenton on Christmas night, 1776. Over twenty years before the Battle of Trenton, the state of New Jersey's first public library was founded in Trenton in 1750.

During the early 1700s, Trenton was the head of navigation on the Delaware. It also became a port for shipping grain and products traveling between Philadelphia and New York City. By 1719, the city adopted the name "Trent-town," after William Trenton, one of its leading landholders. This name later was shortened to "Trenton." Digressing to its role in transportation, Trenton was the main stopping point on the stagecoach line joining New York and Philadelphia. In 1727, a ferry connected Trenton with Philadelphia, completing the transportation circle.

In 1679, the first European settlers arrived in Trenton, when the English Quaker Mahlon Stacy arrived at what he called the "Falls of the Delaware." Prior to the Europeans settling on Trenton soil, the Sanhican, a branch of the Delaware tribe who named the area Assunpink, once occupied the town. The name, Assunpink, meant, "stone in the water" and referred to the rocky falls in the nearby portion of the Delaware River.

Another city in New Jersey that represents part of the Lower Delaware Region's history is Bordentown. Bordentown, located next to Trenton, lies between Philadelphia and New York. The town is situated on a bend in the Delaware River, just beneath a series of rapids where the Delaware is not navigable to large barges and ships.

Before the automobile age during the early 1900s, Bordentown was ideally situated for commerce. Products from

SOUTH JERSEY PORT-CAMDEN

Port of Camden on the Delaware River in Camden, New Jersey.

Photo taken by Jean-Marc Dubus.

Philadelphia, Pennsylvania destined for New York City and further north were transported upriver from Bordentown. There they were unloaded from the ships and barges and placed on wagons for the overland trip to New York. Similarly, goods from New York were brought overland to Bordentown where they were loaded on barges for the trip downriver to Philadelphia.

Founded by Thomas Farnsworth in 1682, Bordentown soon became a thriving trading post for the new colony of Quakers. During the 18th-century, the city's role as a commercial port continued to expand. In the early 1700s, Joseph Borden added a coach line that operated between New York and Philadelphia.

During the early 19th-century, Bordentown became a very important center of trade when the Delaware and Raritan Canal was built for which Bordentown became the southern terminus. Now, products from Philadelphia were offloaded from ships coming upriver at Bordentown, and then loaded on canal barges that went as far north as New Brunswick, New Jersey.

Along with Trenton and Bordentown is a small New Jersey community on the Delaware River named Frenchtown (located 32 miles northwest of Trenton and 50 miles due north of Philadelphia, Pa.).

By the end of the 19th century and well into the 20th century, Frenchtown was a bustling little industrial town, like others along the Delaware. The town, now known as Frenchtown, was once called Alexandria, after one of its original owners and developers. The land was then sold in 1776 to Thomas Lowrey, a speculator from nearby Flemington, New Jersey, who constructed a gristmill and a sawmill. Gradually it took the name in honor of Paul Henri Mallet-Prevost, a Swiss fugitive from the French Revolution who bought the land in 1794. Mallet-Prevost spoke French and the town became known as French's Town, then Frenchtown. Prior to becoming Frenchtown, the area began as a colonial-era transportation center and ferry site across the Delaware River.

In addition to Trenton, Bordentown, and Frenchtown, Burlington, which is south of Bordentown and Trenton in New Jersey, is an historic Delaware River town.

The Dutch first settled in Burlington in 1624. Then shortly after the Dutch arrived, Swedes and Finns occupied Burlington Island, until the English seized it in 1664.

By the fall of 1677, the ship named "Kent" arrives on the Delaware River near the coast of Delaware with English Quaker settlers feeing oppression in England. That is when Quakers were canoeing and walking up the Delaware River to Burlington. By December 1678, more Quakers arrived, as the ship called "Shield" tied up to a big sycamore tree on the riverbank. Shield was the first ship to sail up the Delaware River as far as Burlington, New Jersey.

In regards to seaports, by the mid-1700s, Burlington ranked with New York, Philadelphia, and Boston as one of the busiest ports in America. Burlington was also a magnet for famous and infamous visitors throughout the 1700s and 1800s. These visitors included two late U.S. presidents, Ulysses S. Grant (who lived in Burlington) and Abraham Lincoln as well as the pirate Blackbeard. In fact, many people believed that Blackbeard buried his treasure under a large walnut tree in Burlington.

Rich in historic architecture, Burlington has forty notable buildings, including America's oldest home, the 1675 Revell House; as well as New Jersey's oldest pharmacy, library and Episcopal Church.

Moreover, Burlington is close to the middle of the 110-mile Delaware River Heritage Trail. The trail is a good pathway for riding bikes and walking as it follows the riverfront promenade through the town of Burlington.

Burlington is also home to Burlington Island (a 300-acre island) located in the Delaware River between Burlington, New Jersey and Bristol, Pennsylvania. In addition to being huge, Burlington Island is historic since it became the first permanent European settlement on the Delaware River in 1624.

Yet another historical Delaware River town south of Burlington is Camden, New Jersey. During the early 1600s, the Swedish and Dutch vied for control of the local fur trade in Camden along the banks of the Delaware River. The English settled in Camden in 1620.

In the early 1700s, English Quaker colonists began to reshape Camden. Indians and settlers coexisted peacefully; however, Europeans altered Indian life drastically. The exposure of the Indians to infectious diseases dwindled Indian populations in Camden and surrounding areas.

On the Delaware River on the left-hand side is Burlington Island (located between Burlington, New Jersey and Bristol, Pennsylvania). On the right across from the island depicts the City of Burlington, NJ.

Photo of Burlington Island and City of Burlington was taken by Jean-Marc Dubus from Lion's Park in Bristol, Pa.

Three more towns on the Lower Delaware that represent the river's history are Lambertville in New Jersey along with Yardley and Newtown; both communities are located in lower Bucks County, Pennsylvania.

Lambertville is a city located on the Delaware River in the southwest section of Hunterdon County, New Jersey. During the 18th-century, Lambertville was named after different operators of ferries across the Delaware to Pennsylvania, eventually becoming known as Coryell's Ferry, named after Emanuel Coryell who owned the Ferry. Coryell's Ferry was once the west terminus of the New Jersey part of the York Road (now known as U.S. Hwy. 202) joining New York City and Philadelphia.

The town was called Lambertville in 1814 when the post office was established, in honor of John Lambert, a resident that served as a US Senator and Acting Governor of New Jersey. Yet what contributed to the prosperity of Lambertville were the Delaware River and the Delaware and Raritan Canal. In June 1834, the canal opened and was celebrated with a barge ride from Trenton to Lambertville. Since the 19th century, Lambertville, due to its proximity to the canal, became a factory city where the range of products made went from rubber bands to underwear.

Real estate in Yardley, which is across the river from Trenton, New Jersey, is unique because it offers people many historic properties as well as modern developments. Regarding its history related to the Delaware River, European settlement in Yardley started at about 1682 when William Penn arrived from England with a deed granting him considerable territory by King Charles II in payment of debts owed to Penn's father. William Penn's father was an admiral who helped the King win wars against the Dutch.

How Yardley originated is similar to that of two other Pennsylvania villages, New Hope and Morrisville. Each of the villages developed along the Delaware River where streams were utilized to power mills and by the early 18th century, the villages became focal points of roads and ferries. Furthermore, each of the three communities grew throughout the 18th and 19th centuries with a huge increase in development after the opening of the Delaware Division of the Pennsylvania Canal in 1831. During the mid to late 19th century, early ferries were replaced when each village was

When you look downriver, you will see the Lower Delaware in the center. On the left bank of the river is where Lambertville, New Jersey is located. On the right bank of the river, you will see the Bucks County Playhouse along with other buildings located in New Hope, Pennsylvania.

Photo by Stephen Harris.

connected to New Jersey by means of a bridge over the Delaware River.

But Yardley is also different from Morrisville and New Hope in that it doesn't have the big manufacturing buildings or numerous workers' small houses that accompanied such businesses. Yardley never became a huge milling and manufacturing center.

However, Yardley was the main hub of many transportation lines established in the 18th, 19th and 20th centuries. Also during the 19th century, the town was a significant commercial distribution center for nearby agricultural farmland of Lower Makefield Township, Pennsylvania after the opening of the Delaware Division of the Pennsylvania Canal.

Like Yardley, Newtown symbolizes the river's past. In 1682, Newtown's original 5,000 acres were part of the land parcel bought by William Penn from the Lenni Lenape Indians. During the Revolutionary War, George Washington established his headquarters in Newtown after his famous crossing of the Delaware River. Washington's two famous letters to Congress, in which he describes his win at Trenton, were written in Newtown.

Since 1813, Newtown has been the cultural and commercial center for its nearby communities. Even today, the town still has many historic homes where famous people lived in during the 1700s and 1800s. For example, Quaker Edward Hicks, one of America's foremost folk painters, resided in Newtown from 1780 to 1849. Hicks worked as a sign painter and coach, and painted many local scenes. Today, people can visit his gravesite in Newtown.

Other historic Bucks County, Pennsylvania towns on the Delaware River are New Hope and Doylestown.

New Hope was originally home to the Lenni Lenape Indians, who granted the region to settler William Penn. In 1700, Penn granted 1,000 acres to Robert Heath, with the requirement that Heath construct a water corn mill for settling farmers to use. Heath did so, on Ingham Creek, about a mile inland from the Delaware River. The creek was ideal for milling and more millers set up shop; in time this became the settlement of New Hope.

During the 1830s, New Hope's population increased steadily with the opening of the Delaware Canal from Bristol,

Pennsylvania to Easton, Pennsylvania. As the geographical center of the canal system, New Hope was its main hub.

In 1931, the last commercial boat passed through New Hope, but both visitors and residents still enjoy taking traditional canal boat rides. Since World War II, New Hope has been a friendly and artistic town that safeguards its rural lifestyle.

In addition to New Hope, another historic Bucks County community is Doylestown. Doylestown is located about ten miles west of New Hope. As for the town's past, the 104th Volunteers Regiment was trained at Doylestown during the Civil War when many lost their lives.

By 1792, Doylestown was a colonial stagecoach stop. In 1750, early settlers of the town consisted of approximately six families living in log cabins, a pioneer store, a blacksmith, and the tavern.

Originally, Doylestown was comprised of thick woodlands interspersed with grassy meadows. Two Lenni Lenape Indian trails, one running west/east, the other running north/south, were used by early settlers and eventually widened to become crude dirt roads.

William Doyle owned property at the intersection of these roads, and in 1745, he built a tavern there for travelers. Doyle's business thrived and the crossroads became known as "Doyle's Tavern" that eventually became "Doylestown." Today, that intersection still remains the heart of Doylestown.

Two more historic Delaware River towns in Bucks County that come to mind are Bristol and Morrisville.

Bristol is the oldest town in Bucks County and the third oldest in Pennsylvania. Its Delaware Riverfront looks like a New England seaport because 1917 brought the Merchant Shipbuilding Corporation. That's when shipbuilders and other yard workers poured into town. Then during World War II, the old shipyards were used to build airplanes.

During the 1800s, Bristol's prime location helped make it a busy port and industrial town. Warehouse and coal yards sprang up along the Delaware Canal, as did large mills that made woolens, carpets and other textiles. In 1681, Europeans first settled in Bristol.

Located adjacent to Bristol is Morrisville, Pennsylvania. Named for Robert Morris, financier of the American Revolution, the borough of Morrisville is located at the "Falls of the Delaware River" across from Trenton, New Jersey. Morrisville became a borough in March 1804, the same year the 1,100-foot-long bridge connecting the town with Trenton, New Jersey was erected.

The first mill at Morrisville was constructed from 1772 to 1773; the mills were called the "Delaware mills" in 1780. From 1624 to 1627 Morrisville was used as a major trade route forming a straight line between New York and Philadelphia.

In addition to the history of the Delaware River, human settlers, pre-human period, navigational system, and towns, the history of the Delaware's geology and ecosystem also represent crucial components of the river's history. Its changing landscape also determined and determines how the river was created, what it is like today and what may happen to it in the future.

The wild and scenic sections of the Delaware River System have a great degree of various geological formations that the public can easily access. These geological characteristics provide proof of earth's evolution over an approximate billion-year period and the influence of many significant developments in the geologic history of eastern North America. These developments consist of folding during Appalachian mountain building, volcanic activity, depositional forces, erosional forces, and the intensity of ice age glaciers in the region. Historians claim that the Delaware River was originally established like the path it is on today; a path that first flowed through the Appalachian Range approximately 150 million years ago. In fact, in 1858, the world's first almost whole skeleton of a dinosaur, the megalosaur, was discovered in the area of the Delaware River close to Haddonfield, New Jersey. And at some point in its epic journey through time, river currents in our center-river region started to slice a pass through the Kittatinny Ridge Mountains. The erosion that commenced with running water was millions of years later intensified by a stronger, larger force.

During the last Ice Age (the maximum magnitude of the Wisconsinan Glacier), the Kittatinny Ridge Mountain pass was filled with a 2,000-foot-thick glacier that advanced to the north about 20,000 years ago. The maximum magnitude is an important feature that crosses the Delaware River System. The Upper Delaware is the only massive river that crosses the small lakes portion of the glaciated Appalachian Plateau. Along this upper portion, the Delaware River is made up of glacial and erosional processes that reveal a deep valley with steep relief and moving rock cliffs. Downriver, the glacier scraped its path through the Appalachian Mountain and widened the gap, making the dramatically steep sides on either side of the river. Today, that scenic river pass is named the Delaware Water Gap. Beneath the Water Gap, the river slices through a series of transverse geological formations, including limestone belts, shale (rock formed of hard clay) belts, and the little water Gap at south Mountain. The northern end of the Lower Delaware River and its tributaries slices through the Great Valley section, reflecting the overlapping geology and the growth of the Appalachian Mountains hundreds of millions of years ago, as the Delaware River rolls by the mouth of the Lehigh River at Easton, Pennsylvania.

    The geologic features of the Delaware River Valley support consistent, developed and complex biological communities. In fact, when the Wisconsinan Glacier melted about 18,000 years ago, it left behind a lot of fresh water as well as the gravel and silt (glacial till) that characterized our area's fertile soils thus showing early signs of ecological life in the Delaware River Valley. At about 12,000 years ago, the Delaware ran through an area that was tundra (a widespread, treeless arctic plain) when only the first trees (pine trees) stood close to the river. Then about 10,000 years ago, trees such as birch, oak, maple and willow started to create forests by the Delaware River.

    As the forests grew and widened so did the wildlife. Nearby the river, thousands of birds nested, fed and swam. Mammals, fish, amphibians, and shellfish made a home in the Delaware's currents. Deer, bear, bobcat, mountain lion, wolf, otter, mink, skunk, and beaver all ate food near its banks. Many years later at around the 1600s and years after that, humans settled in the Delaware River Region. Humans changed the river's currents, color, and course as well as its surrounding landscape and ecology. By the late 1800s, a few of the Lenape Indian settlers didn't recognize the Delaware compared to what it was prior to Europeans entering the area.

Aerial photographer Randy Palmer took the majority of the photographs in this book, including the cover photos.

AUTHOR'S SUMMARY

The Delaware River isn't strictly known as an old stream where General George Washington and his troops crossed it (the icy river) from Pennsylvania to Trenton, New Jersey on December 25, 1776 to win an historical battle against the British; it represents much more than that!

In addition to being one of America's most historic and famous waterways, the Delaware is an important natural resource for four states along the Northeastern coast of the United States. The states include New York, Pennsylvania, New Jersey, and Delaware. Unlike many other rivers and streams that have dams, the main stem of the Delaware is quite unique in that basically it is free-flowing. The river is also both a "working" and "scenic" river as it boosts the region's economy yet flows gracefully by scenic mountains, valleys, woodlands, quaint villages, and farmland. In addition, the Delaware River provides crucial habitats to insects, plants, fish, birds, and other wildlife within its ecosystem. Meanwhile, the Delaware Basin provides drinking water for millions of people in the area and gives residents and visitors many recreational opportunities during the spring, summer, and fall. Even in the winter, the Delaware River gives people recreational opportunities. For example, snow tubing is one of a few popular sports at Pocono Mountains, Pennsylvania. In addition, some anglers in the winter travel to where the Delaware flows in New York, Pennsylvania, and New Jersey where they take part in ice fishing.

After people read my book, they will clearly see how the Upper Delaware, Middle Delaware, and Lower Delaware have different characteristics yet each portion symbolizes a critical link to our ecosystem. Furthermore, the river's upper, central, and lower reaches must continue to be clean and healthy so they can maintain the existence of the estuary and all living forms in and along it. Overall, my research on the Delaware and its tributaries definitely enhanced my knowledge of the river. Hopefully, my book will also educate readers about its natural beauty and importance to fish, birds, other wildlife, and humans on a local and national level!

John Bernardo
Author

www.ingramcontent.com/pod-product-compliance
Lightning Source LLC
Chambersburg PA
CBHW050801160426
43192CB00010B/1602